A New Reflection

A New Reflection

CREATING YOUR BEST SELF

Mary Elizabeth Neils

Epigraph Books
Rhinebeck, New York

A New Reflection: Creating Your Best Self © 2023 by Mary Elizabeth Neils

All rights reserved. No part of this book may be used or reproduced in any manner without the consent of the author except in critical articles or reviews. Contact the publisher for information.

This book is intended to offer effective strategies and skills to help create positive change in one's life. It is not intended to replace expert or clinical guidance in healing trauma or mental health conditions. The author and publisher make no guarantee in regards to how much success or change you, the reader, will make by implementing the skills, strategies, and recommendations in this book, as results will vary for every reader.

Paperback ISBN 978-1-960090-13-3
eBook ISBN 978-1-960090-14-0

Library of Contress Control Number 2023907041

Book design by Colin Rolfe

Epigraph Books
22 East Market Street, Suite 304
Rhinebeck, NY 12572
(845) 876-4861
epigraphps.com

To my husband, Joe, and my boys, Joey and Mikey—for their love, patience, and support while I was on this journey.

To you, the reader; you are more than enough! Find your WHYs and soar.

CONTENTS

Preface	ix
Rewriting the Past	1
Forgiveness	4
Behaviors	12
My Story	16
Mind Full	20
Catch That Bus	22
Whys: The Reasons, Explanations, Causes	24
Fear	26
Triggers	31
Strategies to Lessen Triggers/Responses/Reactions	35
Pain	39
Reflection	46
Mistakes	48
Lose the Uncomfortability	50
Re-framing	52
Think Strategy	55
Mind Trickery—Back to the Good Ole Thoughts	60
Self-Talk	63
Sour to Sweet: Changing Thought Patterns	65
Words: Choose Them Carefully	68
Keep Positive and Carry On	70
How: Action Plan	72
Creating a Vision Board, Setting Goals, and Writing a Personal Decree	80

Self-Care: Putting Yourself First	87
Give Thanks and Open Your Heart	91
Open Your Mind: Be the Wildflower	94
Self-Love: Open Your Heart	96
Self-Love Strategies	98
Mindset	104
Emotional Identification: Recap	109
Afterword	113
About the Author	117
Acknowledgments	119
References	121

Preface

Hello, Sunshine, may the beauty of your soul shine brightly and guide your path as you begin this journey to create your New Reflection.

As I sit here and self-reflect—vulnerable, authentic, and transparent are three words I would use to describe where I find myself today. This book has been a journey, years in the making, with many versions and edits as things in my own life have unfolded. My purpose in publishing this book is to reach as many people as possible to remind you, its reader, that you make a difference in this world; you have a purpose and can love the person you are.

Are you looking to stand tall—feel lighter, happier, and empowered—and become the best version of yourself? Then keep reading! As you begin to read this book, imagine you and I are sitting together in a dimly lit room with soft background music. We are comfortably connecting with one another, relaxed and engaged in conversation.

A New Reflection offers simple and effective strategies to help you uncover the best version of yourself and create positive changes in your life. You will be offered the opportunity to do some reflection and proflection, meaning looking back and looking ahead. I recommend having a journal so that you can jot down your thoughts and ideas along the way. There are some suggested activities for you to complete as well. The content about reflective thinking in John Dewey's book, *How We Think*, has led generations of educators and general readers to coin the truism: "We do not learn from experience . . . we learn from reflecting on experience" ([1933] 1960). As an educator, I think of creating your New Reflection with a similar framework to Bloom's Taxonomy (Anderson and Krathwohl 2000), the ground-breaking study that created a universal common vocabulary for defining learning goals: Remember, Understand, Apply, Analyze, Evaluate, and Create. For example, remember by reflecting on experience; understand the why; analyze the how; apply new knowledge; evaluate your emotions; then create a new path to move forward and live your best life.

Throughout this book I will share some of the hardships I've faced, in hopes that this offers a frame of reference for the strategies I provide. I chose to take these experiences and grow from them to become the person I not only strived to be, but was meant to be. Below is a poem I wrote to better explain how I felt before I created my New Reflection. I wonder if you can relate. I firmly believe that if you are reading this book, something will resonate with you to bring about positive change in your life. You will not change what you look at in the mirror; rather, you will change what you see.

NEW REFLECTION

When I look in the mirror
What do I see?
Who is this person staring back at me?
I want to find myself and finally be free.
I can no longer "Let it be."
Invisible tears roll down my cheeks.
Rage builds in my blood.
My smile hides the pain that runs deep.
How is this part of me? Why is it something I keep?
Where am I—who has replaced me?
It's time to stop replaying this reel in my head
And mend the brokenness I so dread.
I'm ready to see my New Reflection staring back at me
By letting my heart and mind be open to the possibilities of being free
And becoming the person I am meant to be.
Proud and passionate about my purpose in this world,
I am a gift, newly opened.
My inner beauty will shine through the shield of armor I wear.
My smile will no longer hide doubt.
I am free, I am ME.

Rewriting the Past

MY STORY began as an adolescent who unfortunately faced hardships that were not processed until later in life. Therefore, these experiences manifested as severe anxiety, panic attacks, and overall dysregulation. This way of living caused me to make very poor choices that were not taking care of my future self. I was always trying to fix something, hide something—or hide from someone or something until I identified that "someone" as *me*, and that "something" as how I dealt or did not deal with situations or experiences. Although you may not be able to change your circumstances, you can change how you act and react. My entire young adult life was spent trying to fix myself rather than accept myself. I had minimal emotional management and absolutely no coping skills to help support me through uncomfortable or negative experiences. I was never mindful of anything I did. I just did. I hope that as you read through this book, you come away with one thing, and that is to not just *do*. You will learn to think purposefully and identify your WHYs. When I speak about your WHYs, I mean the reasons or causes for why you do what you do or did what you did. Why are you ready now to make a change? "If we have our own why of life, we shall get along with almost any how," as was said by German philosopher Friedrich Nietzsche (Kaufmann 2014, 480). You will be able to identify your WHYs and HOWs.

This journey will unlock your roadblocks, hurts, regrets, grudges, or whatever causes you pain and has you stuck. It is time to free yourself of those. How long have you been carrying years of baggage? You can choose happiness or not. I felt my heart was heavy, my mind was burdened, and my body was drained most of the time. My goal is to help you not feel this way. You will be able to take control of your thoughts, create new visions, set goals, identify core values, make connections, practice self-care and self-respect, and love the person you are.

Everyone has a past; each new day makes yesterday the past. Think about this, the past is gone, why bring it back to the present and carry it with you into the future? I am talking about the negative and uncomfortable experiences you want to forget because they bring you down, yet, somehow, they pop up. This is because of unresolved or unprocessed emotions. Whatever you did to yourself or to others, or whatever has been done to you, it is really gone. It will never come back. You will learn to stop allowing your mind to bring it back to the present. Doing so is giving it power and reliving it. I think of this act as feeding the monster. The monster doesn't need to be fed! The first step in the process of creating a New Reflection is to remember by reflecting on whatever caused or continues to cause you distress, strife, and make you feel like crap. You will need to acknowledge them by validating them, and then go through the process of letting them go—releasing the hold you have allowed them to have on you.

Let's Start this Journey

Forgiveness

During this process you will need to forgive. That means you need to drop the armor and ego and let it go. Forgiveness will give you freedom. You must forgive yourself and those who have hurt you. Make amends with them as well as yourself. Forgiveness does not mean forgetting; it means releasing the power you have allowed an experience to have over you that has caused you to feel stuck. Forgiveness can reduce stress and anxiety, and promote strength. It can help move you forward as long as it is your choice to forgive, rather than what someone else feels you should do. It is not about reconciling with someone but about releasing a harmful emotion. Remember there is only one you. You need to take care of yourself; harboring negative emotions is not healthy for your mind or body. The best apology you can give is change.

Before we begin this journey, remember that every experience has an outcome, whether good or bad. Any day, including today, can be the day you or someone you know begins to rewrite their story. We are in control of our thoughts, which generates our emotions, followed by our choices—which typically are our actions/reactions to someone or something. It is important to learn to be mindful of your emotions and the choices you make based on those emotions, while also holding yourself accountable. I want to stress the importance of not playing the blame game or wallowing in self-pity during this transformation. That is a deep, dark hole, and once you are in that hole, it is hard to see the light. You will learn to be your own light when in a dark tunnel.

As already stated, we create our own story. However, the story can change by deleting a chapter, rewriting one, and adding a new one. There is never an abrupt end unless you choose that, and that is what this book is meant to help you with—avoiding the dead ends and getting unstuck! It is important to be able to rewrite your wrongs and, as I stated above, forgive. Without that there is no freeing of your spirit. Avoid blame; it is a word so often used to describe someone's circumstance or predicament, but blame is what can actually make a person become less accountable or responsible. Shame is another feeling that means we feel we did something wrong and are embarrassed by it or ashamed of ourselves. Shame and blame rhyme for a reason, they are usually hanging out together, and you no longer want to be their friend or frequent them. Time to free your soul of these two besties. Be transparent and honest with yourself and others, and you will not have to acknowledge these besties. The feelings of shame and blame can get us caught up in the "poor me" world, so try and avoid going there at all costs. I no longer blame anyone for my hurts or mistakes, and

I no longer live in self-pity. Self-pity is unhealthy; don't wallow in it. It's like the abyss: Once you fall in, it is very hard to get out. Having self-pity can cause one to stay stuck, feeling bad for oneself, clouding perception and causing what I call, *stinkin'-thinkin'*. "Oh, if only that didn't happen to me," or "I was treated like crap—no one cared or helped me when I needed it." Avoid this way of thinking! It keeps you in the negative loop. Experiences teach us something and make us stronger but only if we learn from them, even if it was because we suffered from them.

Childhood is a time when your personality, values, manners, emotions, social skills, coping skills, and relationships begin to develop and then continue to evolve as you grow. What you learn and experience in your childhood impacts you throughout your life. However, when there is a blip in your developmental cycle, and that blip is not acknowledged, it stays within you. So think about a blip as a tiny crack in your foundation (growth), and as you witness several blips (negative or difficult experiences) throughout your childhood, that crack continues to grow and grow until it becomes completely broken (foundation). If that foundation is not repaired and left broken, you will have lived your life trying to repair it or keep it from crumbling. What happens when it starts to crumble is that you react because you do not have the tools to repair it. Good news is, you can make it stronger than ever, even with those cracks. The cracks are what make us who we are and make us beautiful. It's time to acknowledge them and fill them in by repairing them.

Broken is beautiful, especially when you can see cracks repaired. This means it was something important, special, and absolutely worthy of saving. You, my friend, are just that! I love Kelly Clarkson's song from the Ugly Dolls movie, "Broken & Beautiful." Give it a listen, it is empowering. Don't let people try and fix you or make you feel like you need to be someone other than who you are. You are all you need to be. Sometimes we just need to look at ourselves through a new lens, and that is what we will be doing throughout this book.

Are you ready to swim above water and no longer feel like you are treading for hours just to stay afloat? Treading takes a lot of energy—and bravery too. It sucks out your energy and leaves you exhausted. Are you done with the "WHAT-IFs and the WHYs?" It's time to hop off the roller coaster ride—you know, the ones with so many ups and downs, backwards and forwards, loops and twisty turns—and of course, the screeching halts. Please strap in for a transformative ride into the new you. By the end of this book, the person you look at in the mirror will not be the person you see. You will see your New Reflection, created by you. The one you accept, love, and are proud of. Your inner beauty will shine out and sparkle.

Love yourself!

I grew up in what I considered to be a tangled web of dysfunction; however, I only identified this as an adult. Unfortunately, when you live in certain situations you might think it is normal and learn to accept it, because you don't know differently. Visualize a rubber-band ball; that is how I would describe my daily experience. What I knew then was that it was just a normal family life day in and day out. Living in a place of uncertainty, unpredictability, and fear created an emotional tornado within me. By stepping outside of the environment that created this tornado, I was able to also step outside of myself and see things differently. This is what you are doing throughout this journey. Imagine you are watching yourself as you work through memories, emotions and visions. Throughout this journey do not compare yourself or your experiences to anyone else or their experiences; everyone's "normal" varies. What I thought was "normal" was only from what I experienced. You will create your own normal. This journey is about looking at things through a new lens, opening and closing doors as you choose; you are in control of your choices!

"Oh, these thoughts..."

Over many years, I learned more about my day-to-day experiences by reflecting, understanding, analyzing, evaluating, and applying new knowledge to process them. Before I learned to go through this process, I would use defense mechanisms such as suppression and repression. Doing so only adds to the rubber-band ball; picture that in your brain. All those thoughts and feelings tangled together create an unbalanced and unhealthy mind and body. Suppression of thoughts is the act of stopping yourself from thinking or feeling something. It can be good if you are learning to be less reactive—for example, counting to ten before responding angrily to someone, or wanting to say something inappropriate during a staff meeting but keeping it to yourself until after the meeting, when you can speak directly and calmly to the person. However, it is not helpful to suppress speaking up for yourself and getting your needs met. Suppressed thoughts can often be recalled, since it is a voluntary and conscious process, while repression pushes thoughts and feelings into the unconscious mind. Repression can respond to what we will talk about later, which is TRIGGERs and the importance of identifying your WHYs. Repression is often a result of emotionally disturbing or traumatic events. An example of repression is storing an uncomfortable experience deep in the subconscious mind, like an unhealthy experience or abuse. It can cause difficulty later in life, such as toward having healthy relationships, self-worth, self-respect, and appropriate boundaries. Repressed thoughts and/or experiences cannot be accessed by the conscious mind. You have to deliberately uncover them, usually with support, to reveal the memory and/or experience. Deep unprocessed emotional wounds do not just go away on their own. They stay with you and come to the surface when triggered. They appear in the form of mood changes, irritability, rage, sadness, and more.

ACTIVITY:
Forgiveness and releasing emotions.

> *This activity is called "penning." You literally scribble on paper all your thoughts and emotions as if you are writing a letter. You are the only one who knows what is on that paper. You can choose to share it or just rip it up; either way, you are releasing your stored or repressed emotions. As you pen your thoughts, pair this exercise with the statement, "I forgive myself for my past mistakes!" [you can be as specific as you need to be] and/*

or, "I forgive my _____ for putting me down, and myself for accepting it." Identify why you are forgiving either someone, yourself, or an experience, and then try to release the emotions you have kept by not forgiving.

In your journal, either do the penning exercise or write a letter of forgiveness and let your thoughts and feelings naturally flow. Can you identify any blips in your childhood that you never tended to? Write them in your journal. Get out the tools, because it is time to mend the cracks.

Behaviors

Back when I was a young'un, I had very little sense of worth or importance, safety, love, or predictability in my life. I felt lost, alone, frightened and unsure of myself and the world around me. I was always striving to feel better, happier, less anxious, and loved. Unfortunately, it took years before I learned that my own behaviors were, well, my survival skills. To better explain this, I was like a feral animal, scurrying around mindlessly just trying to survive. Monumental mistakes were made because I only knew how to react, fight or take flight, avoid, or just go numb—and that is how I lived my life. What I knew of as typical behavior was far from it. A better word to describe it was atypical, as in actions that are often unexpected or negative and differ from behaviors that are considered of the norm. It was a very precarious way of living. Can you identify behaviors that are holding you back, possibly keeping you stuck? Can you change them by taking baby steps towards self-improvement? How will you do this? Commit to a plan and take action! Use this statement starter: "I will," or "I need." For example, "I will put myself first and need to take care of myself before I offer help to others," or "I need to practice daily strategies consistently to move forward, and I will make that a priority."

Every day is a new beginning, but you must keep moving forward. Avoid bringing yesterday into today, or today into tomorrow. You can learn to close the door and eventually lock it. Think of this journey as a tug of war—you will push and pull several times until you win! Some days you may feel like you are walking a tightrope in trying to balance it all, but you will—just keep your eyes on the path in front of you.

I am a visual person, and for that reason, I will be using many visuals to describe something or explain an analogy. For instance, here is one I thought of while vacationing at the beach. Whatever it is that you want to change—one thing, many things—take it slow. When you are on a journey, you need to walk slowly. Picture this: You arrive at the beach and are so excited to go in the ocean. You drop your things and excitedly run down to the water and jump in. Within a second of being in the water, a huge wave breaks and takes you down. You begin flipping around in the water, panicked, as you try to stand up so you can take a breath. Has this ever happened to you? Or at least, I hope you can picture it. It probably did not feel great due to the unexpected force of the wave that surprisingly knocked you down—making you lose your balance, breath, and control of your space. That is how some of our experiences are, expected and then, well, unexpected! What if, instead, you walk in slowly, feel your toes in the sand, the water gently caressing your body as it begins to adjust to the change in temperature—all while your mind is preparing you to go in further. You take a few deep breaths as you gaze at the sun and feel your toes in the sand under the water, so you take another step in. That is how I want you to take this journey, slow and steady. Give yourself grace and keep joy in this journey. If for some reason you feel like you got knocked down by the wave, get up gracefully, take a deep breath and get prepared to ride the wave next time you see it coming. Keep your eyes open.

By picking up this book you made a conscious choice to make a change to rise up and create your New Reflection, which is the best version of yourself. Every person on this earth is special, unique, and has a purpose. To heal, you must be open, nonjudgmental, vulnerable, authentic, and transparent with yourself. What we see on the outside is not always a true representation of who we are on the inside. I want you to learn to dig deep, as your strength is within. I lived most of my life looking fine on the outside, carrying around a smile, but within me was a beaten-down and broken girl, or so I thought. I recall always being complimented on my smile. It was the one thing I could do well. Today when I smile, it is genuine. I no longer consider myself broken but mended, like a fine piece of broken china that lives on a beautiful shelf in the house with the repaired foundation. Cracks do not have to be hidden.

ACTIVITY:

Choose one or two behaviors or traits that you would like to change and jot them down in your journal. You will be asked to revisit this later in the book, when you set goals. During this journey you must take action and commit, and more importantly, believe that you can do it.

irritability
RIGIDITY
anxiety
FRUSTRATION
CHANGE IS COMING

My Story

TO UNDERSTAND how I can write these words, I will briefly share my story. I am a fifty-four-year-old mother of two boys, ages twenty-two and nineteen. I have been married for twenty-nine years to the most supportive, patient and flexible husband. I was born and raised in Brooklyn, New York with my parents and older brother. When I was twelve years old my family moved to upstate New York, which was detrimental at that age. It was a complete culture shock and caused unnerving loneliness. As I already previewed this, my childhood experiences were like a roller coaster, up and down, backwards and forwards, and always moving in some direction. My parents did the best they could for us, but unfortunately, nurturing was limited. I was only able to realize this after having my own children. I had to learn how to be a parent. My brother and I were exposed to several traumatic events or what I consider chaos. Alcohol and rage were members of our family. As children we learned how to take care of someone and play referee when alcohol became the enemy. God became my closest friend, and I had notebooks filled with letters to God that I had penned, feeling I had no one else to turn to for guidance or comfort. This journey is not about my faith, but without it, I would not be here. I believe my faith protected me, gave me strength, and continues to do so. Find a connection with someone or something that brings you inner peace. We will talk more about these two concepts later in the book.

The move to the country proved more problematic for our family than staying in Brooklyn. My already challenging life drastically changed for the worse. I felt extreme fear and loneliness. Picture this: My parents had a house built in an area with no traffic lights, sidewalks, street lamps, or corner stores nearby. I went to three different schools from grade seven to eight, and when I finally landed in the school district I stayed in, it all went downhill because I was vulnerable and emotionally immature. I had no coping skills for many of the experiences I encountered. I only knew how to react to my feelings in a negative way, so I gave up on myself and ran from the problem. I became my own problem. Sadly, self-sabotage was my escape. For example, I would not think but would just do, and by doing that I would mess up relationships, get off track, opt out of healthy situations, and then just feel bad about myself as the cycle perpetuated. My thinking was the cause of my self-sabotage. Self-sabotage can include either consciously or subconsciously acting in ways that can be harmful and have negative consequences in your life. Most important thing I've learned is to identify and validate your feelings rather than ignore them or let them erupt. Being able to do that will lessen your reaction(s) and provide an opportunity for you to better manage your emotions before they could potentially cause a problem.

During my later teenage years, many things happened within our family and in my own personal life. I began to have increased anxiety and frequent panic attacks. Unfortunately, I did not know what was happening to me because I could not label it. Being an irrational and catastrophic thinker was my default. I experienced intense fear and worry, which controlled my life. It was as though I gave in to it because it was easier than fighting it. I did not know any better, lacked support and felt isolated. I felt unimportant and unloved, and therefore I no longer loved myself. I learned how to fight or take flight, isolate or self-destruct. Can you relate to any of those actions? Just breathe; things can turn around. You will learn how to take power over your feeling of powerlessness by learning to control your thoughts, feelings, and reactions.

I was good at hiding what was really happening. Are you self-sabotaging, hiding behind the curtains and/or making destructive decisions? It is important to learn to identify the unhealthy behaviors and emotions you exhibit and take better care of yourself.

ACTIVITY:

Do you self-sabotage or hide behind the curtain? In your journal, identify ways you may be self-sabotaging. Then identify how such behavior is harmful to your emotional health and what the negative consequences are. For example, do you fear intimacy, love, or rejection—and push away a good relationship; or do you procrastinate because you do not want to deal with a difficult or uncomfortable situation, even though you know it is what is best for you? Do you allow other people to dictate what you need, rather than do so for yourself? Next, identify what steps you can take to change your behavior.

Mind Full

THIS BROOKLYN girl could not get acclimated to the country life. It was so difficult, lonely, and way too quiet. My brother and I tried to keep peace, but chaos always won. My parents really wanted the best for us, and the purpose of moving upstate was to keep us safe because we had experienced muggings, robberies, and other criminal activities in our neighborhood. What they did not plan for was the culture shift—or as I would define it, the shock and challenges of a new environment together with job changes, forging new relationships, commuting everywhere, and having a lot of free and quiet time. I could not handle the quiet. It was so foreign to me that it made me severely anxious, and then my mind would go wild and fill itself up to overcapacity. My mind was routinely full.

Intrusive thoughts, overthinking, perseveration, preoccupation, and rumination: "How do I stop this?" Do you ever just sit back, close your eyes, and ask yourself: "What is going on in my head? Why do I have so many thoughts that are always interfering with my life? What can I do to avoid feeling this way?" Thoughts and emotions create mood. No wonder I was so moody; it was the rubber-band ball living in my brain.

Emotions influence thoughts, decisions, actions, and reactions—and boy, do they exude a lot of control. They are like air-traffic controllers at the airport, telling you the direction to go in and when to take off, wait, and stop. You have to be the supervisor and direct your thoughts just like you would the air-traffic controllers, so they know what they are doing and do not crash the airplane. Thoughts generate our emotions, and they can arise when you least expect it. The emotions of shame, guilt, regret, fear, worry, and resentment are what I consider uncomfortable or negative emotions because they weigh heavily on our hearts and minds and make us feel like we are carrying around a ton of baggage. Without understanding and tending to these emotions, you will continue to carry them, hence the repressed ones. These emotions are working against you. Some days the baggage may feel lighter or heavier, but it is always there. Here's a secret: You can get rid of the baggage. You will be able to stand taller and lighten the load you have been carrying with you. Are you ready to toss that baggage and break free? If you are, read on. I will call this: *No Dumping*—because once you get rid of the baggage that weighs you down, you must not fill it back up again. This journey is about learning to not do as you did but to have a new way of thinking and managing your life. It is realistic to carry around a light bag with just a few things in it, because that's manageable, but do not dump everything in it. Be the gatekeeper and only let in a few items—and not recyclables!

Catch That Bus

LET'S PLAY out a scenario: Imagine you are on your way to catch a bus at your local bus stop and you are carrying bags on both arms. You are breathing heavily and feeling exhausted, but you are focused on getting there on time. You are trying your best and putting forth a lot of physical effort. In the distance you see the bus, so you quicken your steps, but it's definitely a struggle. The bus driver sees you, so he stops the bus and patiently waits for you to arrive. Some of the passengers are gruff and impatient, angrily commenting about having to wait for you.

Here are a few things to think about: You can choose to drop the baggage and run to the bus and get to your destination, or you can continue to feel weighed down and exhausted because you choose to keep all the bags weighing you down, making your experience almost unmanageable. The bags you keep carrying hold repression, mistakes, guilt, anger, trauma, and uncomfortable emotions.

How we act comes down to choices. The people on the bus who are angrily commenting are probably tired from their long day at work, or maybe they have an appointment to get to. But the bus driver sees your struggle and patiently waits, and when you arrive, he greets you with a smile. That is how the world works, everyone is unique and different in how they manage their emotions and handle situations. What you have to do is only be concerned with how you handle your emotions and reactions. It's not about others, it is about you.

So then you climb the steps onto the bus, but the bags are knocking into the seats, and people are getting even more frustrated. You are thankful but embarrassed, knowing some passengers are angry. One gentleman gets up out of his seat and asks if he can give you a hand and helps you place all your bags in the aisle because you cannot fit them in a seat. He also gives up his seat. This stranger knows what's in your bag, because he once carried his own until he learned to lighten his load. He sees your struggle and knows how hard it is to manage them, so he offers support.

Our world is filled with givers and takers. You, my friend, have to choose right now who you are and how you want to live your life. Why are you carrying all that baggage? Why are you struggling in life? Why are you choosing this path? The question remains, WHY?

Whys: The Reasons, Explanations, Causes

LET'S DISCUSS the WHYs. Can you identify your WHYs: Why do you react to certain things the way you do? Why do you hold onto life's challenges and struggles and not *let go*? Why do you feel stuck or uncomfortable in your own skin? Can you relate to any of these WHYs? It's time to be a detective and investigate your individual WHYs. Our emotions, actions, reactions, and choices are all interwoven with our WHYs.

There are many reasons why our lenses are clouded or perhaps stained. To clean them, we must identify the WHY. When I began my journey to heal, I had to dig deep to find my WHY. For me, it was to identify and understand why I always felt like something was out of place as well as why I did certain things and reacted in ways that even shocked myself.

ACTIVITY:

Sit somewhere quietly and identify your WHYs. Write whatever comes to mind in your journal and subtitle that section: My WHYs. You may not be able to answer them just yet, but whatever came to your mind is important to investigate because you have held them in your subconscious, and they could be a repressed memory. Another WHY I would like you to answer on a separate page in your journal is: "Why do you want to create your New Reflection?" or "Why did you make this choice to make a change?" Here are some answers to that question that were shared with me.

My WHYs

- *To be a better mother, father, wife, husband, and friend*
- *To have self-respect and create boundaries*
- *To feel happier and more confident*
- *To reach my potential and achieve my goals*
- *To love myself unconditionally*
- *To live a healthy and optimal life*
- *To forgive*
- *To accept me for who I am—all of me.*
- *To be less reactive and on edge*

Fear

WHEN I began investigating my WHYs, I uncovered fear as a reason I reacted the way I did. Fear is a basic human emotion that is instinctual, to protect one from danger. This led to the discovery that I held a ton of fear within me. I was fearful of the unknown, fearful of judgment, fearful of not being accepted or good enough, and fearful of, well, life. What I also learned is fear is just an emotion you have; it is not who you are. Be observant of your behaviors and see if any could be analyzed and evaluated as possibly being from a WHY. I wanted to lighten the load that I carried daily, and to do so I had to face my fears. What I discovered was that many of my fears were learned fears. Children mimic what they witness. I grew up in fear of everything, talk about living in trepidation! I was young when things began to spiral and spiral downward in my family environment and personal life. Developmentally, I was not ready for the challenges I faced. At the same time, my parents were not equipped with the parenting skills to support me because of their own emotional and physical struggles. What I experienced as a child and teenager made me stressed, irritable, anxious—and was why I reacted to things the way I did.

What a relief it was to be able to identify the causes, my WHYs. Now I could do the work to lessen my fears by understanding, reflecting, analyzing, evaluating and creating positive changes in my life. We cannot go back and change what was, but we sure can change where we are going, and that includes how we act, think, react, and live our lives. As Socrates stated to Alcibiades in the *Platonic Dialogues*, "Know thyself, for once we know ourselves, we may learn how to care for ourselves...." (Taylor and Sydenham [1804] 2016). I learned by using the strategies in this book to stand up to my fear as if it was my opponent in a boxing ring. You will do the same by believing in yourself and confronting fear with your newfound inner strength and knowledge. I use affirmations to help me when I need a little support. Affirmations are positive statements that can help you challenge and overcome self-sabotaging and negative thoughts. One of my daily affirmations is: Strength is within. Dig deep. It's within, but you have to release it.

Fear was my anxiety raging and taking over. It was my insecurities and irrational thoughts that would ignite a spark and immediately become a raging inferno. For example, I remember being so afraid to drive home from work in the dark. I would always think about the "what-ifs." What if I break down? What if someone follows me? My mind would catastrophize a thought into a full-blown fear. The good news is, I learned to talk myself through it, to visualize safety, to rationally think and not allow my mind to think "negative" all the time. These are some of the strategies in this book.

It is perfectly okay to be nervous about something, but it should not stop you from doing what you need or want to do unless it is unhealthy or unsafe.

Rational fear can be helpful at times and can motivate you to do something you have never done before but wanted to do. For example, fear of going on an interview, meeting someone new, or joining a new activity or sport. Separate nervousness from fear by processing it, and that means identify it, understand it, and create a new way to think about it. I call this "thinking with purpose." Once you process the fear and better understand it, you can talk to your fear. Let fear know that you recognize it, and like a lion protects its cub—using your newfound knowledge and strategies—you are protecting yourself from this emotion taking over your mind and body. The more you do this, the less often fear will impact your life. It does not just happen overnight, but continuous validation and using strategies will definitely lessen the intensity of the emotion and how you respond to it. You can run away, but it stays attached to you until you turn around. So look it in the eye and push back.

The truth is out, and now you know I was a scaredy-cat for most of my young life, making more than it really needed to be out of everything. Unfortunately, that was not the only intense emotion I felt. Imagine more emotions filling up a young mind; I was emotionally dysregulated, so I never felt okay, and it really sucked. However, I never searched for the WHY, because I had no idea there could be answers to why I felt the way I did and therefore did whatever I did.

That is why I am sharing my story—so you do not have to live like that. Just knowing ways to help yourself feel better can change your world. When I speak of ways, I mean strategies. I thought everything I felt was me, that something was wrong with me. I had no sense of normalcy. My own behavior added to my dysregulation, often causing it to be worse.

Back to fear for a second. Fear controlled me, and to not feel its wrath I searched for ways to hide it, even if they were unhealthy. Once I identified why I had so many fears, I then had to identify the reactions caused by the fears. For every behavior there is typically some sort of reaction, whether positive or negative. Whatever it is, it is necessary to learn how to control your reaction and manage your emotions in a healthy way. By doing so you are validating your experience while also engaging in effective strategies that will best support your emotional health.

ACTIVITY:

Do you have any fears, and if so, have you ever faced them? Write them down in your journal under the subtitle "Fears." Identify your fear, the cause of it, how it holds you back and what does it feel or look like in your mind and body? Then once you can name it, you can work to lessen it through the strategies you learn throughout the book. Fear can cause both emotional and physical responses in your body.

Create an affirmation that will remind you of your strength when you need it. It is a way to give yourself emotional support and empowerment. Here are some examples:

- *Every day is a new version of me.*
- *Stay Strong and empowered today.*
- *I am absolutely amazing, and my day will be too.*
- *Today is my day!*
- *Be brave.*

AFFIRM IT!

Triggers

TRIGGERS ARE things that cause an automatic emotional or physical response. They are reactions to something. *Things* can be identified as anything—such as people, places, smells, sounds, textures, and so forth. You have begun to identify your WHYs, so now it is time to identify the TRIGGERs. TRIGGERs and WHYs are friends, because they need one another to exist. When I talk about TRIGGERs here, I do not mean an alarm to remind you to take your medicine. I mean things that cause an unhealthy response in mind and/or body, possibly a fear. A WHY (reason) produces a TRIGGER (thing), which causes a REACTION (physical and/or emotional response).

Stay with me as I further explain this through what I consider my own traumatic experience. When I was about fourteen, my mother, brother, and I were driving to my grandparents' lake house in Vermont. My father decided to stay back and not join us for the weekend due to a disagreement with my mother. As we were getting close to our destination, our car slowly came to a halt on the highway. As traffic began to slowly crawl down the highway, several emergency vehicles passed us by. There were many loud sirens and flashing lights.

I remember this experience as frightening and chaotic. I recall being in the back seat of our car, looking around and saying a prayer for whomever was involved in what I was assuming was a bad accident. As we came upon the accident, I remember looking out the window and screaming, "It's Daddy," while making eye contact with my mom in the rearview mirror. Before my mother completely stopped the car, I jumped out and ran as fast as I could to the scene. My father was being placed on a stretcher, and a policeman was next to him. Unfortunately, my father had gotten into an accident with a tractor trailer because he was impaired. He had a change of heart and decided to meet us at the lake house. I remember running to him and letting him know we were there. The aftermath of the accident impacted all of our lives for a long while.

We spent hours at the hospital, then the jail and court the next day. It was a lot for my mom to handle alone as well as for us to witness.

That experience left an imprint on my mind that was extremely frightening. For years, whenever I heard sirens or saw emergency vehicles, I would immediately panic. Telling you about my experience is to help you understand the process I will identify below. My TRIGGERs were the sirens (noise) and the emergency vehicles (sight). Just hearing a loud siren, seeing an ambulance with its light on and fire engines caused me to panic (reaction). The WHY was the experience of not only seeing my dad in the accident but also being present in the midst of the chaos.

So, to go deeper, I stored "uncomfortable emotions" from the experience of the crash that involved loud sirens, police and emergency vehicles. For years, every time I heard the sirens and witnessed emergency vehicles going somewhere it triggered an intense trauma response (reaction) in me. My reactions were fierce emotions and physical responses as well.

I would become frightened, super anxious, irritable or angry, and have trouble concentrating. I remember how my knees would involuntarily shake and my heart would race. I experienced both emotional and physical responses that caused reactions.

To clarify: my WHY was the experience of the accident, the TRIGGERs were the sounds and the emergency vehicles, and the REACTIONs were both emotional and physical responses. The good news is, after delving into my WHY, I was able to use strategies to lessen my reaction to these TRIGGERs. My memory will not change, but how I allow it to impact my life has changed. Identifying and understanding your WHYs and your TRIGGERs is part of the journey of creating your New Reflection. Now that you have identified your WHYs, you can link the TRIGGERs to the WHYs as I explained above. However, once you can identify both, you can use the strategies in this book to reflect and understand, analyze and evaluate, apply new knowledge, and create a new way "how to" manage your emotions.

ACTIVITY:

In your journal, return to your WHYs and reread them. Can you link any potential TRIGGERs that are a direct result of a WHY or WHYs?

Strategies to Lessen Triggers/Responses/Reactions

Your WHYs do not have to be as traumatic as I described above; that was just one of my many "uncomfortable" experiences. Another example could be that you are afraid of heights, because when you were young you fell from a slide at the playground and were scared. You stored that experience as frightening and uncomfortable. Therefore, when you experience heights, you are potentially triggered. The WHY is that you fell and were frightened (reason), and the TRIGGER was the height (thing). Your response, or REACTION, was being afraid and needing comfort; possibly you were crying, your heart was racing, and you scraped your knees or hands. Use this process to reflect on experiences (one at a time) that cause you to be emotionally dysregulated. This is where you need to find time to spend with yourself and delve deep into your subconscious to identify reasons (WHYs) and causes (TRIGGERS) that ignite emotional and physical responses. Your WHY can simply be that you just want to start anew and be the best version of you.

You may not have TRIGGERs or intense emotional REACTIONs but still have a desire for change.

Be patient with yourself, as you may not be able to identify every WHY or TRIGGER, but what you will be able to better manage is your REACTION. For example, when I heard the sirens or saw emergency vehicles, my default reaction was not only to feel the emotional and physical response but also to act, and I would call every member of my family to make sure they were okay. I let fear and irrational thinking take control of me. This was because I never processed the experience or learned how to manage emotions that caused my actions and reactions. Strategies I use when I experience these TRIGGERs are: thinking rationally, using deep breathing, keeping my mind in the present, and talking to my fear. I have stopped myself from calling everyone to check on them, and I have been able to keep my heart from racing and my knees from shaking. I tell myself this is not the same situation, and then I say a prayer. Praying has always and will always bring me comfort and peace.

Once you identify these components—WHYs, TRIGGERS, and REACTIONS of any uncomfortable or traumatic experience—you can work on processing them and rewriting the script in your head that will change the reactions. Use the steps I mentioned earlier from Bloom's: remember by reflecting on an experience; understand the WHY; apply new knowledge; analyze and evaluate your emotions; then create a new REACTION by using strategies. Prepare yourself before you react, and you will be less startled when the TRIGGER pops up like a jack in the box. You can also stop the thought by using self-talk, visualization (picture a flashing stop sign), and deep breathing.

I want to point out that if you have a difficult time identifying specific TRIGGERs, just begin to notice when there is a drastic change in your emotional or physical response to something and jot it down. As they arise, keep a log of when and where they show up. Once identified, you can work on lessening your REACTION by using the strategies above and those discussed further in this book. Quieting the mind, providing it with clarity and rationalizing your thoughts—along with giving yourself inner peace, choosing acceptance, and staying in the present—will benefit your overall well-being.

We will refer back to your WHYs and TRIGGERs after we identify strategies to use when you experience them. The strategies we will discuss can be used for almost anything you experience that makes you uncomfortable. It could be that you are having a bad day, or meeting with someone who makes you uncomfortable, or having to go somewhere you would rather not. Strategies are like tools to keep in your toolbox. You will have a variety of them to use when you need them. It is important to use them consistently so they become part of your behavior. Always show yourself compassion, which is paramount in this process.

ACTIVITY:

In your journal, you have identified your WHYs. Now go back and identify your TRIGGERs and REACTIONs. Then identify how you can better manage them with strategies. Use the following format.

- *WHY: Identify the reason, cause of the memory/experience, or circumstance.*
- *TRIGGER: Identify the thing that reminds you of the WHY.*
- *REACTION: Identify the emotional and physical response(s) to the TRIGGER. Use strategies to lessen the trauma response. (Identify what those are.) You can revisit this page and add and change things as you identify and practice strategies.*

I am in control of my **THOUGHTS, ACTIONS, & REACTIONS**

Pain

WE ALL have layers of pain that we can begin to peel away to reveal our true selves. These layers are experiences, possibly ones that were never acknowledged in a way that allowed them to be processed and validated so they could no longer affect us. These layers have protected us by keeping in the hurt as if trapped behind a locked door, but in actuality these layers have kept you from being who *you* really are. To rid yourself of these layers, you will need to identify them. The practices you just went through are just the beginning of opening up your mind, allowing yourself to identify and release the feelings buried deep within your heart and soul. These buried feelings are the deepest hurt that has caused you pain, and that pain has tainted your life experiences, which has kept you from being who you are meant to be.

Most uncomfortable feelings come from a place of pain. However, we do not have to carry them with us wherever we go. Drop the baggage. You can lessen the power pain has over you. I have deep faith, and God saved me more times and in more ways that you can imagine. Believe in something greater than yourself, whatever that may be, during this journey. Everyone experiences pain but the pain I am speaking about is the kind that hurts deeply and leaves a wound. Physical wounds need healing—but so do emotional ones. When you are hurt physically, you get a Band-Aid, or stitches, or may even go to a hospital to be taken care of. But what about when you are repeatedly hurt emotionally? How do you get help, who takes care of you? If your emotional wounds are left untreated, they can create significant emotional dysregulation and inner suffering, which can cause lives to be disrupted. This can be from living in what I call an emotional tornado with no way out, always waiting for it to lose its power before you come out to safety.

Emotional wounds left untreated are just like a bad infection that needs antibiotics to heal. The infection affects your heart and mind and leaves you physically and mentally unhealthy (wounded). Think about anger for a minute, the kind that causes the rage to build up in your blood. You can physically feel it, and then the emotional tornado erupts and hurts whatever or whomever is in its path. Anger is a reaction to something. That, my friend, is from years of not tending to an infected emotional wound that still needs treatment. Can you identify any triggers (thing) that cause that reaction? Knowing the WHY and processing it will lessen the power of the REACTION if you experience that feeling again. Remind yourself that it was *then*, in a different time—and you are safe, strong, and no longer affected by that original experience that caused the pain. Remember to talk to that person in that original experience and tend to his/her needs, show love and empathy towards that person (*you*). The good news is that it's never too late to tend to those wounds. The first step to healing is identifying those emotional wounds, and then you can tend to them. You are stronger and braver than you think! So, let's get started.

I use the word *wounds* even though you cannot see them, because they're there and they hurt. When you face an experience that is a TRIGGER, you probably immediately react, and often without thinking because it is opening up an untreated wound. All things can be mended with intention.

Now, you don't have to sit and list all the hurts and bad experiences in your life that caused you pain. Those of us who have faced trauma and continue to have TRIGGERs causing a trauma response can use this strategy to help get unstuck in those situations. You will have a renewed mind. Changing the way you feel inside will change the way you are on the outside, the beautiful person you really are. It's like a fixed mindset versus a growth mindset. When you have a fixed mindset, you stay stuck and default to attitudes like, "nothing will get better, it is what it is, I am the way I am and that's it." This way of thinking is limiting and can keep you stuck. A growth mindset is thinking positive, being open, and having flexible thinking. You default to, "I can do this, although I may not be able to do it yet." Having a growth mindset allows you to identify new things, see things differently, accept new ways, see others' perspectives, and grow. If you are interested in learning more about mindset, there are several well-researched books on this topic. The opposite of trauma is blessing, comfort, contentment, happiness, and joy.

My hope is that you will begin to feel these comfortable feelings with your new mindset! You are in the driver's seat—in complete control of your direction, thoughts and actions, challenges, boundaries, goals, and future. You are not in control of your past or other people's actions, reactions, and lives. We cannot change other people—only ourselves. Within ourselves, we can change our actions and reactions.

At age sixteen my life began to unravel. My parents divorced and I became withdrawn. My mom struggled emotionally, due to the circumstances she faced. Coping skills in our house were reactive and volatile. How I handled my emotionality was definitely not with helpful or healthy measures but with destructive decisions. Unfortunately, I knew only how to react. Later, I learned that my behaviors were responses to the trauma I had never processed and still continued to face. When I look back on my life, I did not care enough about myself. I had limited coping skills or strategies to use to move myself forward and manage my life. I did not know my WHYs. I was on a perilous journey. As I have grown, I became determined to shift these unhealthy dynamics by learning and developing strategies to not make destructive decisions and share them. Creating change in your self-care strategies takes intentionality and effort, and over time this effort will help you create your new reflection. These intentional choices become healthy daily habits.

When I was in graduate school, I learned a lot about my family history from the research I conducted. I learned about my family genetics, traits, medical history, culture, and family systems. This newfound knowledge finally shed light on my WHYs and gave me the answers I needed to understand why things happened the way they did in my life. What I learned was disheartening but, at the same time, validating. What I uncovered was that my mom was raised primarily by her grandparents. Her mother worked full time in the city and was a single mom. My mother never knew her father and was given no information about him, although she tried to get answers. My grandmother was overly critical, and my mother lived her life trying to please her mother. My father was one of seven children and lived with both parents. He also faced several hardships during his young adult life. His younger sibling tragically passed away. My dad struggled with severe anxiety. Unfortunately, he was not diagnosed until very late in life after turning to alcohol to help him cope.

My younger sister, Sharon, passed away after she was born. My mother fell ill after her birth and devastatingly never got to meet her baby girl. Sharon was buried by St. Vincent De Paul Catholic Charities. My brother and I found out about Sharon when my father released his suffering after enjoying a few cold brews. I was thirteen. The secret they kept was out, and that brought up many repressed-hidden feelings. My mother was emotionally fragile, never having been provided with grief counseling or support. Back then, it was as though she was expected to get up and go on. And that is what she did. She carried guilt and resentment for most of her life. My point here is that it is helpful to know your family history because it can help identify and explain your WHYs, not just for yourself but for your family members as well. Being able to understand why my mother reacted the way she did also gave me an opportunity to understand and support her. Knowing your family's WHYs will help you identify and understand circumstances, experiences, actions, reactions, choices—and yourself, overall. It helps clean the clouded lens you have been looking through. I hold absolutely no resentment towards my parents, and I love them with all my heart. I like this quote by James Allen: "Circumstance does not make the man; it reveals him to himself" (1902, 15). I am grateful for what I've experienced because it taught me so much about myself and gave me a desire to be a helper in this world.

My brother and I had free reign of the house more often than not. This was pretty cool back in the day, but in actuality it was a bad idea. Why? My house was *the hangout.* I cut school, hung out, and used alcohol, myself. I followed the crowd and that's what everyone around me was doing. I never felt comfortable in my own skin. I thought what I was doing was the norm because I neither knew the difference nor had anyone to tell me otherwise. I now had an identity, and more importantly at that age, I had friends who came at a price. Going back to self-sabotage—indeed, that is what it was. I needed guidance at that age. Part of this behavior was that I did not have goals, hobbies, confidence, or dreams—and I felt very alone. My advice to you, whether you relate to these feelings or not, is to do things that matter to you and help define you. I regretted those years of my life and felt ashamed and disappointed in myself until I put together the pieces of my puzzle. I was then able to grow and learn from those years, so that they did not define who I was but actually helped me become who I am. During this time of my life, I did not know why I did what I did, I just did it to survive. Do not just accept where you are and try to fit in, stand out! Progression is not perfection and memories take us back, but strength carries us forward.

My brother went off to college, and then I was alone. Up to then, we had each other when things were difficult. He definitely protected me and my mother as well as our home. Unfortunately, he had to return home from college not by choice. During those years, I was caught in several unfortunate situations where I felt paralyzed and numb, and I blamed myself. I carried these uncomfortable, repressed feelings into my adulthood. But ultimately, using strategies and having a new mindset allowed me to drop the baggage I had been carrying for years. Like the bus scenario, I am finally able to catch the bus when it arrives. Memories remain, but how you identify and process them can drastically and positively change once you commit to making a conscious shift in your thoughts, actions, and reactions. So let's talk about our good-ole thoughts. Think positive and believe that you are meant to do great things. Do you know what makes you happy, do you have a passion you want to pursue? Write these down in your journal.

Reflection

As you continue reading, let's take a minute and connect. I want to make sure you feel my words, "You are important, valued, worthy and you matter in this world." Get up and clean your mirror, it's time to see the beginnings of your New Reflection that you are creating. Think of having a blank canvas and you are in the process of painting a magnificent self-portrait that highlights your awesomeness.

Trauma is defined as a deeply disturbing or distressing event. There are different types of traumas: Acute trauma is a single event, chronic trauma is repeated and prolonged, and complex trauma is exposure to various and multiple traumatic events. I faced complex trauma. No matter what, trauma is devastating and changes you—but it does not have to define you or keep you stuck. Everyone who faces trauma has different reactions to it. Some reactions are quiet and internal, while others are strong and intense emotions along with physical symptoms. These reactions within the mind and body are the responses to the trauma. The neurotransmitters in your brain are activated and send a message to your body, which causes a physical response. Hollywood's legendary martial artist and actor Bruce Lee once said that you can lose yourself by giving in to emotion, because the mind always leads the body.

I will teach you my THINK strategy to help better manage your emotions and reactions to either TRIGGERs or just uncomfortable experiences we all face on a day-to-day basis. This simple acronym is an effective strategy which will ignite a script in your mind identifying what you have learned and how to proceed to remain calm and in control, taking care of yourself.

ACTIVITY:

> *Here is a quick activity: Stand in front of a mirror and gaze at yourself for a minute, keeping your head high while relaxing your shoulders. Now, take your hand, place it on your chest and gently pat your heart as you say out loud, "I am important, valued, worthy—and I matter in this world." You must be nonjudgmental and open-minded. Write this in your journal. Repeat this daily or create your own daily mantra.*

Mistakes

MISTAKES! WE all make mistakes. I am built from every mistake I ever made—a multitude of them. I'm sure you have heard the saying that mistakes are only mistakes if you do not keep repeating them. I do not agree, because I made the same mistakes over and over because I lacked the ability to cope with them. And rather than acknowledge them, I would figure out a way to just forget them. I never processed them or thought them through. This behavior caused even more anxiety. My advice is to acknowledge your mistake by taking the time to process it, then forgive yourself but learn from the mistake so it isn't repeated. Mistakes are hidden lessons.

There is always a reason for a mistake happening in the first place; it goes back to the WHY. Understanding and acknowledging the WHY will prevent the mistake from reoccurring. Learning to be a purposeful thinker will bring you inner peace and allow you to live in the moment while actually thinking about your action or reaction to a situation or experience. You will become way more aware of what you are doing while you are doing it—because it is your choice, you are in control. Everything we do has a reason (cause) and reaction (effect). Never feel rushed to make a decision that could be irrational. It is okay to tell yourself or whomever you are with, "I need a few minutes," or "I'm going to need to get back to you on that," or "I am not sure and need time to think about that." Give yourself time to process what is happening. I hid the feelings I had from the mistakes I made and this negatively affected my life. I felt ashamed and disappointed in myself, which then made me feel worthless because I hid these feelings as fast as I could, like blowing out a candle. Mistakes are actually teaching tools; they teach us what we can do better as well as what to never do again—but only when we process through them. Decide to move on and begin again. Can you identify any mistakes that you regret or have kept you feeling bad about yourself? It is helpful to own them, apologize if needed, to yourself or someone else and forgive. Free your mind, it is not a monthly paid storage unit.

learn from your mistakes

Lose the Uncomfortability

IT'S TIME to rid your mind of any lingering uncomfortable emotions you have kept for far too long. These feelings have held you down and kept you from being the best you. They can trap you in a downward spiral when they resurface. If you do not change your reaction to them, you are allowing them to take over, control your mind, and cause your reactions and behaviors. Changing how you react to your own feelings can lead to a whole new way of living. As Robert Frost wrote, "He says the best way out is always through." (1917, 66). It is time to do some more self-reflection. As I mentioned above, experiences, whether good or not so good, leave imprints on your mind and in your heart.

So far on this journey, you have identified your fears, forgiveness, whys, triggers, reactions, and mistakes. You have begun to peel back the layers where these things were hiding, toss them once you have gone through the process of remembering, understanding, applying your new knowledge, analyzing and evaluating the emotions attached to them while creating your best self.

LOSE THE UNCOMFORTABILITY   51

ACTIVITY:

In your journal, identify what you have learned about yourself ("I am _____.") and what you want for yourself ("I want _____."). Put it out there and manifest it.

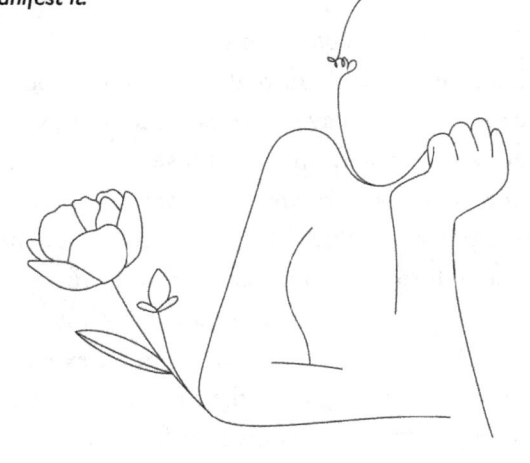

Re-framing

LET'S GO deeper with this. Thoughts have emotions attached to them that create our moods. For every experience we have there is a thought generated, and emotions arise from that. Those emotions are stored in our minds with the memory of the experience. To live a happier, healthier life, one must change the negative, uncomfortable emotions attached to thoughts from an experience that was, let's say, troubling and unpleasant. As a result, if we have a similar experience in the future that brings back the memory that was stored as negative, these emotions resurface. The brain does not differentiate between the two experiences, even though they are different. You need to learn to override the brain's response by reframing the thought and emotions attached to the original experience. This is not saying to lessen the emotions you had of the original experience but to not let these emotions have power over you that, in turn, negatively affects you. This is what I do when I experience a reaction from a TRIGGER caused by an uncomfortable memory, just like the flashback I shared regarding my dad's accident. You can reprogram or rewire your brain. This is known as brain plasticity, meaning your brain is malleable. Not to get too scientific, but there are two types:

- Structural Plasticity—experiences or memories that change a brain's physical structure;
- Fundamental Plasticity—the ability of the nervous system to change its activity in response to intrinsic or extrinsic stimuli by reorganizing its structure, functions, or connections.

This means that the brain can be shaped, molded, or altered. Scientists believe that the brain stops growing after childhood, but it can change through reorganization. New learning and experiences can cause new neural pathways to strengthen. You can reprogram thoughts attached to difficult memories by revisiting them and reframing the emotions attached to them.

I have done this several times, revisiting the child in me and taking care of her in order to heal as an adult. In some circumstances you have to go back to move forward. This process takes a bit of work; however, it is a powerful process towards change. I revisited experiences that still affected my life. I knew they did because of TRIGGERs I had, so I referred back to my WHY and then continued through the process of understanding them and applying new knowledge to move through. This process enabled me to no longer let them have an effect on my emotional well-being. It's perfectly okay to talk to the person you were during that experience. Remind yourself (the person you were) that this is your life now, and you are moving forward. Use positive self-talk to identify your strengths and reframe the feelings you attached to that experience. You can give that person (yourself) what you needed then, be compassionate and empathic to that person.

Next, we will explore a strategy I use almost daily. Using it will help keep you in the present, stay emotionally regulated, and lessen your reactions. I mentioned it earlier—it is the THINK strategy.

Think Strategy

WE ARE all thinkers, you can be an over thinker or a quick thinker, reflective thinker, obsessive thinker—and, well, there are many more types of thinkers. I am going to encourage you to learn to THINK with purpose. Seriously, *yes!* You need to learn to THINK about everything, because there is a cause and effect for all you do. I was on autopilot for years and just did things without thinking and then had to deal with the consequences of my poor decisions and actions. Why didn't I take the time to think about things more? I could have spared a lot of suffering and time if I had actually thought first before doing. I was mindless in my actions. Can you relate? Here are two ways to remember to think and be mindful of your actions and reactions by using your new strategies and knowledge when you feel stuck or uncomfortable. I use the acronym *THINK* (see the meanings below).

> *THINK:* **T**ransformation **H**appens *when you* **I**mplement **N**ew **K**nowledge. *(That is what you will be doing when you close this book.)*

Take **H**old **I**mmediately **N**ow **K**nowing is an effective strategy to use when you catch yourself being reactive and upset due to uncomfortable emotions. When you use this strategy, you are teaching your brain to think differently. Stop yourself and reframe your thoughts, knowing you can control them and not allow them to default to old behaviors that held you down. I use these measures when I catch myself reacting because I did not thoroughly and purposely think about something. I remind myself that I have coping skills and strategies that I can use to help myself get through situations or change the narrative and remind myself that I am okay. I talk to myself using positive self-talk. Positive self-talk is a very powerful and readily available calming and empowering strategy. There are times when I catch myself being overly emotional and switch my thoughts by saying, "THINK". This brings me to the awareness that I need to lessen this reaction. Even if it is something justifiable and my reaction is appropriate but I want to calm myself, I can because when I tell myself, THINK. It reminds me to Take Hold Immediately Now Knowing I can emotionally regulate and give myself what I need to move through these emotions and new experience.

To keep it simple, here is just one common example of what I call an absence thinker not being observant or present in the moment. Have you ever parked your car in a parking lot and ran into a store—and once you got out of the store, you forgot where you parked? That is not thinking about what you are doing, because perhaps your mind was already preoccupied with other thoughts. If you think with purpose and stay present in the moment, you would tell yourself, "I am parked near the light," or just take notice of what is around you, like taking a picture (nonverbal thinking). This same example pertains to all experiences and how one processes thoughts, whether verbally or nonverbally. So the feelings associated with you not knowing how to locate your car were probably anxiousness, embarrassment, and frustration.

However, it was also a lesson for next time to slow down and process what you are doing because you don't want to feel that way again. Your body and mind will remember that experience and the feeling you attached to it. So, once you find your car, tell yourself, "THINK: **T**ransformation **H**appens when you **I**mplement **N**ew **K**nowledge. My new knowledge is that I need to be present and pay attention in the moment to what I am doing. This will allow me to remember where I am parking so I do not experience this uncomfortability again." Learn to be mindful, taking notice of what is around you and processing the thought. However, if when you finally found your car, you put yourself down and were anxious or angry, then you would store the experience as a negative and uncomfortable one. If this ever happens again or something similar occurs, your mind will default to those negative feelings because that's how you stored them. Hence, there is a TRIGGER (misplacing the car). The negative critic will show up and tell you, "You're an idiot. You never pay attention." I catch myself—before I allow the negative critic in or react inappropriately—by telling myself, "THINK: **T**ake **H**old **I**mmediately **N**ow **K**nowing," meaning I know how to cope, reframe my stinkin'-thinkin', and show compassion to myself and others. It is about rewiring your brain and how you store your thoughts and feelings from experiences. You are changing the narrative, which is exactly what you tell yourself. If you ever experience something like it again, that negative feeling will strike like a cobra hiding in the tree unless you have processed it and stored it without an uncomfortable feeling. It could even be acceptance, owning it, and forgiving yourself. This happens with traumatic memories/experiences as well. When TRIGGERS bring them back to the present moment those feelings resurface, unless you reprocess them and reframe the original thoughts and emotions attached to them (refer back to TRIGGERS).

Change your reactions by learning to no longer be self-critical; rather, be self-caring. This process is about changing the default, meaning where your mind automatically goes. Just learn to catch yourself, begin by being mindful of your thoughts and feelings and moving through them, so when a similar experience happens, the narrative is different. Use the THINK strategy and let that be your new default (key word) when you catch yourself with uncomfortable feelings or just need a reminder that you need to take hold of yourself because you now know how important you are and how to better manage your emotions.

Thoughts that are processed meaning (identified,

validated, analyzed, and understood) are typically rational, with better outcomes than thoughts that are not. The non-mindful, what I call absence thoughts, as mentioned above, are the quick, impulsive, reactionary, and often irrational ones because they were not processed with purpose. These non-mindful, mindless thoughts keep us spinning, causing a negative outcome. It takes a conscious effort and daily practice to THINK purposefully. If it is not something you currently do, it will take time to become automatic. It is important to learn to sort your thoughts rather than have them in one large heap that you are always trying to unravel, like my visual representation of the rubber-band ball. This is not only exhausting but also overwhelming. Who needs to feel like that on a daily basis? Try to stay in the moment and be observant of what you are doing. Conscious change is a process that encompasses awareness and acceptance.

Mind Trickery—Back to the Good Ole Thoughts

MY MIND tricked me into believing whatever I thought. My thoughts were exaggerated and irrational, which caused me to perceive reality inaccurately. I was a negative thinker, and that seriously affects your self-esteem and everyone around you. These thought patterns are called cognitive distortions, which means distorted thinking. Once you become aware of them and understand the WHY for having them, you can begin to shift them when they arise. Sometimes we are so hyper-focused (meaning an intense form of mental concentration that focuses consciousness on something) or hyper-vigilant (meaning overly conscious about potential threats or danger), that we may not even recognize how we are acting, because it is what we know as normal or "how I am."

Once I learned about these thought patterns, I was able to catch myself and shift my thoughts. There is no doubt that my thought patterns resulted from exposure and learned experiences. There were many cognitive distortions, and my mind let them in as if they were good friends. I will name a few here, but if you feel your mind does this as well, read more about them.

I would experience the cognitive distortion known as "all or nothing thinking," meaning everything was either always or never, great or horrible. For example, if I was nervous about something, I would think negatively to think my way out of it: "There is no point in doing this," or "I'm not going—no one will talk to me." Without evidence, I would jump to conclusions thinking every outcome was going to be negative. If it wasn't perfect, in my mind it was horrible. This type of thinking causes low self-esteem, self-worth, limits self-acceptance and keeps you stuck. It also affects the people around you. Have you ever been around someone who is negative and it drains you? Avoid falling in their trap. It goes back to being a fixed thinker or a flexible thinker. You become what you think!

I also used something called emotional reasoning and labeling. This means I believed every emotion I had to be reality. I was such a negative thinker and believed every negative thing I heard as if it was guaranteed true, with absolutely no evidence that it was. I absorbed it all like a sponge. I mentioned this earlier as *stinkin'-thinkin'*. It keeps your mind in a negative loop.

Cognitive Behavior Therapy is a form of therapy that is very helpful in identifying and learning how to shift your thought patterns. I highly recommend looking further into this type of therapy if you are a thinker like I was. It helps you identify unhelpful thoughts and behavior patterns. I suggest keeping a thought record in your journal and begin to notice what type of thinker you are. The more aware you become of your "thought world," the easier it will be to catch yourself and change your thoughts to be healthier and more positive.

Self-Talk

OUR THOUGHTS affect the way we experience our daily lives. They initiate the internal dialogue we have within ourselves. This is our inner voice. Use your inner voice to speak kindness to yourself and work towards keeping your thoughts positive. Self-talk is an awesome strategy to use and has many positive benefits. It is a natural cognitive process, and you need nothing to do it other than your own mind. It is readily available to use as a coping skill/strategy to support you emotionally. It is an internal dialogue you have with yourself to help you face challenges, increase confidence, slow down, problem-solve, and process your thoughts—all of which engages the brain. It is a way to think more optimistically and feel empowered. It can help reduce stress, improve self-esteem, increase vitality, and improve mental health. You can talk to yourself silently or out loud. I use this strategy multiple times a day and often get caught talking to myself. Using this strategy has helped me slow down and become a good and effective listener, and you can too. Examples of positive self-talk are:

- I am strong and confident.
- I can do this even though I am nervous.
- I'm proud of myself.
- Breathe deeply and relax.
- I am in control of my actions and reactions.
- Stay Strong.
- Keep it real.

> *When things change inside you, things change around you!*

Sour to Sweet: Changing Thought Patterns

LET'S PRACTICE changing your thought patterns by reframing negative thoughts to positive and powerful ones? You have been working on this already in the activities above. Well now, we want to see if happen. Remember your body mimics your mind. It is time to connect your mind and body. Back to the mirror. This may feel really awkward to you at first, but please give it a try. How you actually see yourself physically can affect how you feel emotionally. Fix your eyes not on what you see but on what you do not see. It is time to bring out your inner beauty.

ACTIVITY:

Set a timer for five minutes. It will feel like eternity, but hang in there. Try to do this in front of a full-length mirror or in a way where you can see most of your full body. Now stare at yourself. At the end of the five minutes, jot down in your journal what you saw and felt through this exercise. Limit it to five things. Were your thoughts negative and/or self-critical?

Draw two columns titled positive and negative. Choose a negative or unkind thought you had about yourself and turn it into a positive one. Learn to become self-caring rather than self-critical. This exercise is about changing your thoughts and the way you look at things. For example, I wrote down: "I can't stand up for myself. I have no confidence". I changed that negative unkind thought to be positive and empowering. I wrote, "I am strong, confident, and my opinion matters." The more we acknowledge our own irrational thoughts (not logical or reasonable and usually negative) and change them to rational (logical, reasonable, and often positive), the better we will feel about ourselves. You are important, and you matter. Change the narrative in how you speak to yourself.

If you had a negative thought like this, "I look old and tired." Maybe that is how you feel at that moment because you work hard and are exhausted, but begin to notice the good even in why you may feel that way. So rather than seeing yourself as old and tired, see yourself for the reasons you may feel that way and change the thought. "I see the beauty in my smile that spreads joy to others." Take hold of positive thoughts and use them daily. This purpose of the exercise is for you to learn to give yourself the same kindness and compassion I am sure you show others. Use "I" statements: I feel, I am. For example, "I feel kindness is seen in my eyes. I am smart, strong, and brave!"

The reason I asked you to view most of your body is because our bodies tend to respond to our feelings. If I feel old and tired, I probably slouch my shoulders, keep my head down, and create what my words tell me.

Notice this as well, your body reacts to your thoughts. When you turn the negative to positive, watch your body language change. You will stand taller and keep your head up. It is important to tell yourself these positive thoughts, so tell them out loud while you are looking at yourself. The more we give ourselves kindness and compassion, the more alive and vibrant we will feel.

Here is a narrative I wrote after doing this exercise a few times. I was finally able to see what my eyes could not:

> *I am not my past mistakes or hurts, but I am stronger because of them*
> *I have risen above them as I have climbed mountains and braved storms*
> *My mind is a clean slate and I am ready for my transformation*
> *I am more than enough*
> *I feel happy being me*
> *I am in control of my thoughts, visions, goals, and dreams*
> *I love myself unconditionally*
> *I will keep healthy boundaries as I hold the key to who enters and exits my life*
> *I am stepping out of my circle with confidence and viewing the world with a new lens*
> *I am proud to be me*

After completing this exercise a few times, gather all your kind words and thoughts and create your own narrative in your journal.

Words: Choose Them Carefully

VISUALIZE YOURSELF at a carnival. You are walking past the games and come across the one with a temporary wall filled with colored balloons. You decide to play and are given six darts. You must throw the darts one-by-one and try to pop the balloons. If you pop a few, you win a prize. Well, some people do just that, they say hurtful things (darts) until you explode or they know you are hurt. As messed up as that is, it happens. Do you do that to yourself as well?

Continue. Think about these balloons as your heart and the darts as words. Have you had words thrown at you that hurt so bad, you're scarred. Have you done this to yourself by repeating those words over and over again in your head, believing what you heard. When you hear those trigger words, do you burst like a balloon (react) or do you just accept them (suppress)? You can reprogram your reaction. This time, imagine the dart just tapping the balloon and bouncing off. It cannot puncture it—you are as strong as that balloon. Words hurt, but they do not have to burst you. Also, when the words are coming at you, change them. If you find yourself saying unkind words to yourself, stop (visualize a hand signaling stop or a flashing stop sign) and self-talk, "I am not what my mind is telling me right now. I am _____." Use your renewed mind. Words, I mean verbal hurt, stays in someone's mind, including your own, far longer than it takes physical wounds to heal. Choose your words wisely and with intention. You are the gatekeeper and can unlock the door and let them in or keep them out, it is a choice.

Keep Positive and Carry On

MORE ABOUT Words! Words carry so much meaning, and I can bet that there are times you probably just use words without actually thinking of their meaning or intent. Have you ever just spewed words when irritated or upset and then caught yourself and thought, "Oh, shit!" I often used the same words so much that they no longer had the meaning they were meant to have.

Learn to choose your words. In today's society we are taught to process everything so quickly, and we often do, but it is perfectly acceptable to take a few minutes and think before you speak, especially when you know you need to. For example, I would always use the word, *worry*. I would say things like, "I will worry about that later," or "I'm so worried about that," etc. Just by changing the word, *worry*, I changed my perception. I simply replaced *worry* with *process* or *think*. For example, "I will think about that later," or "I will process that further." The words you use can set the mood for the day. Using *worry* already sounds negative—why worry about it rather than handle it later or just do it later? Worry robs time. It does nothing for us, it is useless. Just speaking negative words out loud to yourself keeps in the negativity. For example, like we recently talked about, if I look in the mirror and say to myself, "I look old and tired." That sets me up for not feeling good about myself before I even get started on my day. Instead, I could say, "I am beautiful and ready for my day." Keep it positive and you will undoubtedly have a better day. Research indicates that positive self-talk and self-love absolutely boosts the feel-good hormones: serotonin, dopamine, and endorphins. Stop clinging to old ways, patterns, and habits. Begin each new day speaking kindness to yourself. Do the following, replace:

- I can't with *I can,*
- I should with *I will,*
- I'm not with *I am.*

How: Action Plan

IT'S TIME to strategize the HOW to create the best version of you. You have identified your WHYs and the desire to make positive changes in your life. Imagine being stuck on an island alone, but you have all the skills and attributes needed to survive, what would they be? How will you survive? These attributes are part of your HOW. How can you do anything?

Just as you had many WHYs, you may have many HOWs to answer. Everyone will have at least one. For example, you may question, how can things change? How can I forget the past and move forward? How can I love myself as I am? How can I walk away from toxic people and environments? How can I have that career? How can I become a leader? Choose your HOW. The HOW can only be answered by you taking *Action*. Here is another way to remember that. **A**ct **C**onfidently **T**owards **I**ndependently **O**wning your **N**ow. Meaning, be strong, believe in yourself, own it and go for it now. I remember as a young cheerleader the chant, "Action, Action, we want Action." Rather than just want, you must do!

Let me share with you one of my HOWs—how things changed for me. One morning during high school, I was called out of class by a monitor who told me my mother had come to school, and I was wanted in the guidance office. I was scared and mad at the same time. When I turned the corner, I saw my mother. I was confused and angry. She was there because she was mandated to be there. I was cutting school and my good grades had turned to failures. My parents had never come to school before. I was escorted, like a criminal, to a lady in our school that everyone had labeled as the meanest one of all. I remember thinking, "What is going on here?" It all started in English class during my tenth-grade year. My white-haired, quiet but kind teacher would greet me every day at the door with a caring smile. He saw me daily for one class period. Over the course of the year, he noticed something changed in me. I was a good student, but that year, well, I began to cut school and not do my work and was completely disengaged. He went to administration with his concern for me, and in turn they went to the in-school suspension teacher. She, at that time, was a private counselor for children of alcoholics. All I could think was, how did he know? No one knew that anything was wrong. I was fed, clothed, had working parents, and thought I was doing okay. This encounter was the change I needed. It also showed me that people cared about me, and without judgment, I mattered to them. After this meeting with the "meanest lady of all," the one positive change was that my family started therapy. That became problematic and did not last, but thankfully, I stayed with it. My family life did not change, but how I dealt with situations did. I was taught to not only identify my feelings, but to also actually feel them, manage them appropriately, and use strategies and coping skills to support myself whenever things became too overwhelming. I learned my WHYs and created my HOWs.

Today, things are very different, in a good way, since I was in school. I am thankful for my teachers back then, but now we have additional support staff in schools. Teachers are so in tune with their students that they build relationships with them, and by doing so, know when to refer them to support staff like me or check in with them more often. Children are all so unique. As a former teacher, there were two types of students I was drawn to. There are the quiet kids who sometimes fall under the radar, and the defensive kids who stand out.

The defensive kids are typically the mouthy, outspoken, disruptive ones who act out. They are probably that way because that's how they learned to cope with life from exposure and/or learned experience. These students are always ready to attack—protecting themselves from the hurt, or pain, or put-downs—feeling inferior or judged and having a difficult time allowing anyone in. They need time to develop trust and feel that the teacher is genuine, trustworthy, and not superficial or manipulative. Teachers who do not give up and continue to spread kindness and compassion for them even when they are not showing their appreciation, make a difference. It takes longer to develop this with kids who experience or experienced trauma and lack of coping skills. These students grow up to be adults, and without a change in behavior they will continue to be the same and probably will have relationship problems, will be unable to hold down a job, and will struggle with their emotional regulation. The only way change can occur is through recognition, trust, accountability, and acceptance.

The quiet kids are just the same but learn to withdraw and isolate to protect themselves. Some days and in some classes, these children (individuals) can be the quiet one, and on other days, the defensive one. "To love is to be loved," and they may not have experience with that emotion, and it feels fake. Kindness can feel foreign and even make them angry until they begin to allow it in. It will happen, I know, I was that kid. As you age, you learn to take care of yourself both physically and emotionally, but your first experience with this is when you are a child and taken care of. If you were not nurtured and cared for as a child, you have not learned how to emotionally regulate as to why you exhibit these behaviors. Do you know someone like this? Is this you? Once an individual can open their heart and allow in compassion and love, they will feel a sense of belonging and connection. Through working with students over the years, I have been blessed to be able to see myself in their reflection, and therefore, I not only deeply understand but also empower them to be their best self through recognition, trust, and acceptance—along with a will to change. Behavior has to be recognized and accepted before any change can occur.

Back to my story about working with this lady who I will refer to as Mrs. P. She helped me work on myself and identify who I really was. That meant I had to dig deep. It is amazing how much you can learn about yourself. I actually loved talking to Mrs. P., as she empowered me, helped me find my identity, and changed my life. I was fortunate enough to locate her a few years ago and thank her for all she did for me. I let her know what I had accomplished with my life. That felt amazing! I also want to recognize my high-school bus driver and all bus drivers. I cannot remember her name but she always smiled at me and made me feel safe and comfortable every morning. So, thank you for doing what you do and letting students know they matter. Teachers, all school staff—make a difference in the life of a child each and every day. If you are a teacher or any staff member working in a school, you make a difference by greeting your students, connecting with them each and every day in some way, and reaching out when you know something is off. It's more important to be proactive than not active at all. Sometimes all you need is someone to connect with, someone who believes in you, has compassion, and likes you for who you are. That's what I needed then. As a student, this level of compassion will carry you through a rough time at home just knowing that tomorrow you will see that person who makes you feel like you matter. We all matter!

Who has been a positive person in your life? A friend, coworker, teacher, family member? Go ahead and write their names down. What can you do to let them know how you feel? You can make a difference in their life. Go forward and, in your own way, acknowledge them.

I graduated from high school—I did! Off to work I went. I started working at age fourteen, so it was natural that I continued. College—that was never a discussion in my home. I actually wanted to work and help my mom, because she supported us. My guidance counselor specifically told me I would not get into any colleges, and going into the workforce was my best option. I remember the day, what the office looked like, what she looked like, and where I was sitting when she told me. However, I felt differently. You can listen to what other people tell you, but you have to listen and believe in yourself too. She was probably right to say that, knowing my educational history, but I knew I was better than what I had given myself. My belief is that no matter where you come from, who you are born to, or what you experienced, you have a purpose in this world. We all have roots but can grow in many different directions. Anything is possible, at any age. It is never too late to create a New Reflection. As I remind myself daily, "Stay grounded where your feet are planted and grow in the direction of the light." Take a minute and identify your light.

I eventually went to college as a result of meeting my first boyfriend, who was in college. This relationship positively changed my life. I believe he was placed in my life for a reason. He had a strong family unit, and I was able to experience this by spending a lot of time with them. This helped me see what a functional family was, learn deep values, gain self-respect, and understand how to love and be loved. Without his entering in my life when he did, I do not think I would be where I am. I believe my journey may have taken a different path.

College also changed my life, and I absolutely loved it. Although I had severe panic attacks in class and high anxiety driving to and from class, I had strategies to help me manage them. I was able to openly talk about my feelings and/or experiences and reach out for support when I recognized I needed it. By doing so, I learned there are many people that experience these same feelings, as I did. This helped normalize what I experienced. I was a straight-A student, on the dean's list, honors every semester, and even made it into *Who's Who in American Colleges and Scholarships*.

What a climb from where I was at the very bottom in high school! I went on to be an elementary education teacher, a special education teacher, and currently, a school psychologist. I also found my hobby and love of fitness. I became a fitness instructor, personal trainer, and nutrition coach. I even won a national aerobic championship. If I had not stepped outside of my comfort zone to forgive, reflect, identify my WHYs and HOWs, and use strategies, I would never have accomplished what I have. Anything is possible, but you have to believe in *you* and put in the work. You have to want it, because no one can carve your path but *you*. I am forever grateful for who I am and have become, but that did not come without failure, mistakes, regrets, and a river of tears. However, these feelings turned to resilience, perseverance, grit, and a will to succeed. You have to make a conscious choice to change. The reality is that it is not always going to be easy, but it is worth it. You are worth it! Remember your daily mantra, "I am important, valued, and matter in this world. I am enough." Repeat those phrases!

ACTIVITY:

> *Identify your positive attributes and write them in your journal. Use them to assist you in creating an action plan towards change? The one WHY I asked you about is why did you want to create a New Reflection? The next section has a few activities that encourage you to delve deeper into your new identity.*

Creating a Vision Board, Setting Goals, and Writing a Personal Decree

IN THIS section, you will complete three activities. These activities will offer you an opportunity to look inward, identify your character, and plan your hopes, dreams, and future goals. They will also help you with your HOWs.

CREATE A VISION BOARD:

Do you remember that question you were asked in school year after year, "What do you want to be when you grow up?" I could never answer it. I never felt like I wanted to be something, because I just wanted to be better than I was. I never revisited that question until I was much older. Unfortunately, it was never a discussion in our house; there was no future planning or investment in what we would become. As a child I was uncertain about the world—let alone, myself. There was always something taking my attention away, and at times, it was myself—my own mind. I always had an escape plan or created fantasies just to manage getting through each day. I was constantly seeking answers or trying to problem-solve from a very young age. What I realized early in my career was that there were many children who were never asked these questions or encouraged to look forward, dig deep and create their identity. This is where you have the opportunity to revisit previous thought provoking questions and identified behaviors to help you engage in these activities.

Creating a vision board allowed me to see what inspired me, what I enjoyed and what were my hopes and dreams. I filled my vision board with powerful words, affirmations, pictures of my dreams, my inspirations and likes, my goals, and role models. I encourage you to create one and keep it somewhere you can see it on a daily basis. You are never too young or too old to have a vision for yourself, and it can change as you change. No one should or could tell you that your vision is unattainable, because you can do anything you want with passion and heart. It all starts there. Passion never fails! I never thought I would do what I've done or had the perseverance and grit in me, but I did. You do as well! In full transparency, I barely graduated high school, but as I shared earlier in this book, I attained the goals I set.

Affirm what you desire. You are strong and capable of trekking on through this journey, so let's have some fun. It's time to create your best self/new identity. What are your visions, dreams, aspirations, values, desires, and challenges? It is time to look inward and reflect on what you want to accomplish in your life.

This activity is about proflection, which is the act of progression and moving forward—visualizing what you want to bring into existence through pictures as if you were creating a picture story for yourself. Think positively about what you want. Some questions you can ask yourself are: What do I aspire and want to pursue? What qualities do I want to develop? What are my dreams? How can I make a difference? What would the answers to these questions look like?

ACTIVITY:

> *Now grab your journal and write down your thoughts. When you have time, create a vision board with words and pictures, highlighting these things or whatever is important to you. This visual representation will be a daily reminder of your life's vision, goals to achieve, values to live by, dreams, and whatever you desire and is important to you.*

SET A GOAL:

If you can't see it, you can't be it! Do something you never thought you could do. Spend time thinking about this and choose something you want to achieve from your vision board. Set an action plan by writing a goal to achieve it. Make sure you are specific when writing your goal. It must be realistic and attainable. This is where you will plan your HOW. For me it was running a half-marathon, getting a second master's degree, and writing this book. Manifest it and do it! Step out of your comfort zone and show yourself that you are capable of doing more than you think.

Setting goals is committing to something and it incorporates your thoughts, emotions, and actions. Give yourself a realistic and attainable timeframe to achieve the goal. Share your goal and find a support system, or group as well. This can help with accountability. Through social media and community organizations there are many groups you can join that have the same interests and desires as you. Spread your wings and fly.

GOAL—**G**o **O**ptimistically **A**head **L**earning. Without a plan, a goal is just a goal—no more, no less. Create an action plan by specifically identifying the goal. Create steps highlighting how you are going to do it. Identify any roadblocks and plan the detour ahead of time, get an accountability partner, monitor how you are doing—and, if needed, restructure it. For example: I will run a half-marathon in six months. I will train four days a week for one hour in the morning. I will follow a specific marathon training plan. I will join a running group on social media and share my progress with others. I will eat healthy and avoid all processed foods. Obstacles: going out to dinner (I will look at the menu and plan ahead); and bad weather (I will go to the gym and run on the treadmill). Always have a backup plan ready. Here is a template you can use as a guide for your goal-oriented action plan.

GOAL: What do I want to achieve?
ACTION PLAN: How will I begin?
- What are the big steps I need to take to begin?
- What are the little steps I need to take to begin?
- How often will I monitor my progress towards my goal?
- What will my backup plan be if I hit an obstacle?
- Who will I share my goal with?

ACTIVITY:

In your journal, plan your goals and write a detailed action plan using the above suggestions. However, choose one goal to work towards at a time. Remember step in slowly (the beach scenario)

WRITE A PERSONAL DECREE:

Here is another activity to complete in conjunction with creating your vision board and goals. It is another step in declaring your identity.

ACTIVITY:

In your journal, identify your beliefs, core values, and how you choose to live your life. Then gather the ones you feel are most important and write them down just like a testament to yourself. It can be a few sentences, to an entire page. Use "I" statements. It's time to declare it. Write it down, frame it, share it. Here is an example of one:

> *I will practice daily gratitude and spread kindness to all.*
> *I am worthy and deserving of love and connection.*
> *I will give and receive unconditional love.*
> *My family, self-respect, love, honesty and faith are paramount in my life.*

*I will keep my heart open and my mind free
of negativity and judgment.
I will live in the present and be mindful.
I will achieve the goals I set and celebrate
my accomplishments.
I will love the person I am!*

Keep this in a place where you can see it often. It will help you stay true to yourself and set boundaries so that you can consistently achieve what you set out to do. Identifying these things can only be done by looking inward. Through these activities you have now identified your visions, goals, strengths, core beliefs, values, and what is important to you. This is YOU!

Self-Care: Putting Yourself First

I LOVE helping people in a healthy way, but for most of my life I sacrificed myself and my time for others. I was altruistic, which again was what I considered a survival skill. I had to take care of the people I loved before I took care of myself and my needs. I've learned that you can be altruistic while also being codependent. This means having: an intense focus on others' needs, suppression of one's own emotions, and the desire to fix other people's problems. I thought I was helping but later came to realize that, instead, I was enabling that person. I focused on other people's needs, wanting to fix their problems while suppressing my own emotions because I thought it would make things better. I lacked trust in myself and had poor self-esteem, so helping others made me feel better about myself. This behavior comes from the belief that other's needs are more important than your own. It is a behavior that affects your ability to take care of yourself, and keeps you from reaching your potential because you are so focused on other people and needing them to be whole. It leads to poor relationships, lower self-esteem, and poor decision-making. If you feel you may be doing this, stop and think and ask yourself, "Am I actually helping or hurting others and myself? What can I do differently?" Self-care should be your priority.

I also became way too independent in my young adult life. It was a struggle for me to let people in or even allow someone to do something for me without thinking they had a motive. I would automatically feel inferior and think: I am not enough. I should be able to do this. Why do they want to help? Am I a failure? I took care of myself, but at the same time I neglected my emotional needs and relied on other people to make me feel good. NO! NO! NO! Learn to put yourself first! That does not mean to suddenly be selfish; rather, it means to not lose sight of yourself and your needs. You can give yourself what you need instead of seeking it elsewhere. Learn to live with balance.

> Do you provide other people strength, causing
> you to be tired?
> Do you give compassion and love to others to
> provide comfort?
> Do you sacrifice your needs for others?
> Would you do the same for yourself?
> *The strength, compassion and love you need to give is
> your own.*

Self-regulation is a skill that we all need to have. It allows us to regulate our emotions, thoughts, reactions, set goals and self-reflect. If you struggle to self-regulate, you may have trouble concentrating, staying present in the moment, remaining in control of your actions and reactions, and managing your life. Without it, you may feel distress and unable to think rationally. When this happens, you cannot problem-solve or make good decisions, because your mind is like the rubber-band ball, and a chemical rush fills your brain, causing the impulsive, or "default," reaction. Self-Talk, deep breathing, taking a break, writing in your journal, and physical movement are a few calming self-regulation strategies.

Co-Regulation is the same process but with another person rather than one's self. It is helpful to have a support system—someone you can trust who can help you if you need support through this journey. Co-regulation is a process between two people that aims to help manage immediate emotions and foster self-regulation. One nervous system calms the other. This is a process that provides emotional relief to both parties. Think of it as looking at the reflection of the calmer person and learning to model their self-regulation, and it will help rewire your brain and renew your mind.

So, who are you? Can you feel your words written earlier in your journal that identified your awesomeness (strengths and positive qualities)? Can you begin to see yourself for the greatness within you, the love you have given, all that you have done in this life thus far, and how you are admired. Focus on the positives and let them knock down the negatives like no-fail dominos. Sometimes all you really need is someone to believe in you! You can be that someone. Find and feel the good in you—be proud of who you are, do not hide behind the curtain, get out and stand at the front of the stage.

ACTIVITY:

Think about what someone would say if they were to give a speech about you, and write it down in your journal. Now read it out loud. How does it make you feel? Is this how you want to be known or remembered? Now that you have identified your strengths, use them when a weakness pops up in your mind. If you have not done so yet, write them down where you can see them. Here are a few strengths I often remind myself of.

I am worthy—

I am fierce—

I am smart—

I am enough.

Give Thanks and Open Your Heart

DIGGING DEEP to identify who you are includes being thankful for who you are. Research shows that gratitude can actually increase the neurotransmitter serotonin, making you feel good. It can also improve sleep quality, increase happiness and positive emotions, reduce stress, and improve your overall health. Practicing gratitude should be a daily practice. What is gratitude? It is showing an appreciation for someone or something. What are you thankful for? Having gratitude will open your heart and keep it open.

```
    I   a m
 g r a t e f u l
```

You may have heard this saying, "A heart is a magnet for miracles." Keep it open, allow yourself to feel. Do you go against compliments or just not agree with others who share how awesome you are? Do you experience self-doubt? Take the compliment, really listen to the words someone speaks to you. Do you always listen to the negative and let it soak in like water absorbed quickly in a sponge? Well, it is time to change that and do the opposite by letting the negative be like oil, so it is not absorbed and soaks in. As I was going through my healing journey, allowing love in was something I had to practice. I had become so independent that I was like a robot, on autopilot. I never stopped to feel. This ties into the war I had with myself where my words or anyone else's did not match my feelings, and there was a disconnect. Have you ever experienced this? Do you randomly say something using a feeling word, but in actuality you do not really feel it? I could talk a good talk, but deep within my soul I was not feeling it. I knew I should, but I had to learn to let it in. Keep your heart open. Let in what you may have shut out and let in the good. I thank God every morning and every evening for many things but primarily for giving me another day and guiding me to be the best I can be, even when I make mistakes. When I place my feet on the floor every morning that is my cue for how blessed I am to be given another day. When I lay my head down on my pillow, no matter how hard the day was, I inhale gratitude and exhale grace because I know I did my best. Always keep your heart open.

ACTIVITY:

I suggest either keeping a gratitude journal or creating a gratitude box. Every day, write down what you are thankful for, either in your journal or on a small sheet of paper to be placed in your gratitude box. For the first few weeks do this for yourself, meaning that you will identify what you are grateful for within yourself (part of your self-reflection page in your journal). After a few weeks, extend out to other things, people, and experiences you are thankful for. For example, I am grateful for the sun shining through my window this morning. Share your gratitude. How you view yourself and the world will begin to change over time, and with that, so will your experiences—just by showing gratitude.

Open Your Mind: Be the Wildflower

During an outdoor run with my friend, I had this thought come to mind. We were running outside an abandoned factory, and the concrete parking lots had many cracks in them. In the cracks were these beautiful purple and yellow wildflowers. I was completely drawn to them because they were so vibrant in color and pretty to look at. These abandoned but precious flowers grew out of brokenness and made me realize that even in the midst of damage, something beautiful can grow. You can be just like that flower, strong and vibrant. I had this occur to me on another occasion and want to share it with you so you can experience the same thing I did.

I was out walking my dog along a path near a quiet, serene, and gently flowing creek. I came upon a beautiful wildflower growing on the edge of the creek. I was captivated by its beauty and went down to take a closer look. This flower inspired me. I noticed it was among the weeds, but it stood out—tall, strong, vibrant in color. This flower has been through storms and changes in water levels and temperature. Yet it stands tall and beautiful, beaming with strength. Wildflowers represent strength.

ACTIVITY:

Go out and take a walk. What do you notice in nature? Look for the wildflower. It is amazing what you can see when your mind is open and free. There are signs everywhere.

Self-Love: Open Your Heart

KEEP YOUR mind and body healthy. There are so many SELFS, like self-worth, self-efficacy, self-esteem, self-confidence, self-actualization, self-doubt, and so on. Just be yourself. The two most important SELFs for this transformation are self-love and self-care. The only SELFs to avoid are self-critical and self-doubt. That is not to say you should avoid critiquing yourself. There are times you may need to look inward and work on some things, but you can do so in a way that is not critical, which will only limit you from being your best self.

As I have grown and my roles have changed from daughter to wife, mother, aunt, friend, teacher, school psychologist, personal trainer, fitness instructor, and nutrition coach—I finally found the answer to another important WHY. Why did I want to create my New

Reflection? My answer is to love *myself, all of me—not just what I look at—what I see, inside and out.* It sounds so simple, but you have to love yourself first before you can love anyone else. To truly love yourself, you have to rid yourself of baggage, accept who you are, and have hope for where you want to go. To move forward, you have to be nonjudgmental, vulnerable, transparent, and authentic. When you make a mistake, accept it, own it, and move past it. Forgive yourself. When you are wrong, just admit it. You are not in competition with anyone, so why be that way with yourself. Keep your heart open and allow love in.

ACTIVITY:

Reread your personal decree, look over your vision board, and stay true to your purpose on this journey. Reread your I AMs and deeply connect the words to your heart. Love who you are! Every now and then you will go off the path and possibly fall in a ditch, but remember to see the light and crawl back out to it. Hope is never lost, and every day is your day to love yourself. On a blank page in your journal, draw a large open heart like the sketch. Take a few minutes and sit quietly with your eyes closed and ask yourself, "What do I love about myself?" Open your eyes and write the first five words that came to your mind inside the open heart. Every morning, look in the mirror and say these words to yourself. For example, I love you [your name]—you are kind, smart, helpful, creative, and loving.

Self-Love Strategies

Here are a few strategies you can use to give yourself compassion, kindness, and the unconditional love you so deserve.

HUGGING OTHERS:

Are you the cold-hugger, where you get stiff and barely move when getting or giving a hug? Or an over-hugger, where you hold on and squish the person you're hugging? Are you someone who hates to be touched, because it feels so uncomfortable that you want to jump out of your own skin.

Well, you may want to give it a try and be just a hugger. Hugging can decrease the release of cortisol, which is a stress hormone, and blood pressure—allowing your body to relax. It also provides a feeling of safety, love, and comfort if you allow it to happen. Touch is very powerful and can deactivate the *fight or flight* feeling. It also releases serotonin in the brain, which is the feel-good hormone that helps us feel happy, calm, and confident. I learned all about hugging in one of my graduate classes. We had an assignment where we had to increase the amount of time in which we hugged someone. At first, it felt so unnatural and awkward, but the more I did it, I realized it gave me a sense of comfort that I really enjoyed. I am not saying to go hug strangers, but do hug those you want to hug, with their permission of course. The more you do it and allow in the "good" feelings, the more natural it will feel.

SELF-HUGS:

Have you ever given yourself a hug? Self-hugs are comforting and provide you with a sense of security and contentment. They are just as powerful and effective as deep-cleansing breaths to relax you. Try it. Here we go—stretch out your arms, cross them in front of you while taking a deep inhale, and as you begin to exhale, wrap your arms around you, close your eyes, relax your head and neck, and tell yourself something kind while giving yourself a pat on the back or a strong and secure squeeze. If you are not really into self-hugs, get a comfy pillow or stuffed animal and give it hugs. Hugs release a happy feel-good hormone, whether you are giving it to yourself or someone else. Pair the hug with a cleansing breath and a positive statement. I like to hug while closing my eyes, inhaling a deep belly-breath, and as I exhale, I think a happy, positive thought. Sometimes during this practice, I also set an intention for the day.

CUPPING:

I termed this strategy as "cupping," which is not the kind that people use to increase blood flow in the body; rather, it is simply cupping your hands as if you were holding your own hands. I do this when I am in deep thought or having to make a decision, problem solve, feel nervous in an uncomfortable situation, or just need comfort. It reminds me that I am strong, brave, and worthy. Try it. Here we go—cup each one of your hands as if you were trying to hold a small amount of water in them and then put one hand on top of the other. They will fit together like a puzzle. Then you can rub your thumbs across your hands. It is a beautiful gesture to yourself and a reminder that your thoughts are connected to your heart and that you love yourself.

CONNECTION:

Connection is a feeling of belonging. When you are living in a vulnerable place and searching for connection, you may ride that roller coaster and take risks, not knowing what is ahead. Who and what do you connect with? Check in with your visions, strengths, and values. Are you connecting with anything, anyone? I've learned to connect and reconnect with many things. I love to write, paint, hike, run, and dance. Is there someone you enjoy being with, a place you enjoy going, an activity you enjoy participating in? Make a connection and act on it. Doing things that bring you joy and happiness will add to your overall good health and well-being.

ACTIVITY:

In your journal identify what brings you joy? Is there something or someone you can connect with. Can this be tied into your goals? Can you add it to your vision board?

BREATHING:

Focused and intentional breathing can cleanse the body and help clear the mind. It can reduce stress and anxiety. There are many breathing techniques. I personally like belly-breathing. Give it a try and lie down on your back in a comfortable position. Let your muscles relax from your head to your toes. Place one hand on your belly and the other hand on your heart. Inhale through your nose and fill up your belly with breath, seeing your hand rise. Now slowly exhale out of your mouth as you see your belly deflate and your hand lower. Do this a few times as you let your thoughts enter and exit as you remain relaxed. You can add to this moment by visualizing yourself in a peaceful place, relaxing and connecting with yourself. You can also practice mindful breathing where you simply focus your attention on the breath coming in and going out.

INTENTIONS:

Set an intention every day upon waking up. Another way to connect your mind and body is to ACT (Allow Connection of Thoughts). Feel what you desire. For example, my intention for the day is, "I will smile at each person I see today," or "I will be patient today." In doing so, begin to take notice of how you keep your intention as well as how you respond to others. Awareness is also noticing your own behavior and how it impacts others and how others' behaviors impact you. There is also a positive connection with others, as there is within your mind and body when setting and following through on intentions. When setting daily intentions be sure to keep them simple, specific, and positive. We often go about our day, managing through varying emotions without acknowledging, validating, or identifying them as we discussed above. Once you change your internal dialogue, your external world will change as well.

INNER PEACE:

Daily self-reflection will increase your self-awareness and ability to find inner peace. Inner peace can be thought of as a deliberate state of psychological or spiritual calm, despite the potential presence of stressors such as the burden arising from pretending to be someone you are not. It allows you the ability to enjoy each moment without judgment of yourself or others. Even when obstacles come, you can experience them as nonthreatening and proactively work through them, walking a calmer and clearer path, now knowing you are in control of your thoughts, actions, and reactions. If you feel at any time that you are defaulting back to your common reactions, breathe and simply remind yourself to return to the present, and use the Think strategy. *What brings you inner peace?* Delve deep, do some introspection and find out. I enjoy prayer, meditation, journaling, exercise, and dancing.

When you reflect, you think deeply. Every evening, reflect on your day. Accept whatever comes to your mind, give gratitude and grace to yourself, and provide hope. Reflecting will offer a new way to view yourself and the world. Do this before bed; it also helps declutter your mind. This practice will help you sleep soundly with a clear mind and an open heart, so you can dream big! You can make this a nightly journal practice.

Mindset

LET'S REVISIT Mindset. You are in control of your thoughts, and unfortunately it is not as simple as it sounds to "just control them." Life is exhausting at times, and when you have to work to control your thoughts, sometimes it is just easier to let them speak, although it can often be negative or overwhelming. However, in the long term, the more you allow them in, the more power they have. Do you allow irrational or negative thoughts to throw you into a tailspin and cause discomfort? Does the negative critic come knocking at your door and let itself in? Do you allow it to hang around and talk too much? What do you do with those thoughts? You can welcome them in, but then let them back out so they no longer weigh you down.

You are strong enough to change your thoughts from irrational to rational and from negative to positive. I use what I call "guide words" to help me when I get caught up here. I tell myself, "Switch." That means, change my mindset. We all get in moods, but you can also get out of them using these strategies. Why stay there? It never feels good. Take a break if you are feeling crappy, it's okay to say, "I need a break for a minute. I need to clear my head and open my heart." It is learning how to change your mindset, so it does not default to what you know or what you are used to doing.

Having a malleable mindset will allow change, and change by choice is healing. How we think, as I mentioned above, is how we feel. Our reactions come from the feelings attached to those thoughts. People who know you will identify you by the experiences they have with you. For example: "She is so thoughtful and kind." "He is so negative and impulsive." We develop our perceptions, values, personality, and grit from our experiences. This is why we need to reflect and learn from them so we can be the person we are meant to be.

ACTIVITY:
Peaceful place

> *Visualization—This exercise should be done with an experience you have already processed but you want to let go. It could be one that just pops up from time to time but hinders your overall well-being. This activity will allow you to release the negative feelings once associated with it.*
>
> *You will use your senses to create a peaceful place in your mind that you can visit and revisit at your discretion. Okay, let's get started. Begin by getting yourself in a relaxed and comfortable position. Relax your body while taking a few deep cleansing breaths. Inhale (1-2-3) through you nose and exhale (1-2-3) out of your mouth. Inhale strength and exhale doubt.*
>
> *While settling in, keep yourself relaxed and*

comfortable. Allow your breathing to remain slow and steady. Begin to visually create a picture of your peaceful place. Using your senses, identify the following things: What do you see? What do you hear? What do you smell? What do you taste? What do you touch? For example, my peaceful place is a beachfront lake house. I am lying on a soft, colorful beach blanket close to a lake, my toes are in the sand, the wind is blowing softly and the birds are chirping. I smell the crisp, cool air, I gaze up at the beautiful blue sky. I taste the peppermint mint in my mouth. Now imagine you are handed a pen and a piece of your favorite-color paper. Go ahead and write down one word or a few words that describe the experience you want to let go of and release from your memory.

Staying relaxed, begin to crumble the paper into a ball and visualize a bird or, in my case, a seagull (they grab anything you give them) flying down, picking up the ball of paper and taking flight carrying it far, far away, to never return. Now repeat, "I am no longer affected by _____ [whatever you want to release]." Then repeat a powerful statement showing your inner strength. I like to use this one: "I am strong, I chose to release _____ from my thoughts. I am strong." This is very powerful and can release the deepest hurt if you allow it to go.

Once you have completed this exercise, if the thought of the experience ever returns, visualize the bird carrying it away—separate from you, gone. Talk yourself through the release, for example: "I released you, and you have no more power over me." Like I said before, this takes practice, but it works. I use this strategy whenever I have any negative thoughts or feelings creeping up from the experience. I knock them down like a prize fighter by repeating the phrase I attached to my release. I can do so because I have already processed and validated the thoughts and emotions from the experience. Think of the bird as a catalyst to help you soar and be free.

The Peaceful Place visualization strategy is also effective to use when you just need to calm yourself, take a break and reset. I love visiting my peaceful place and use it for relaxation without visualizing the bird taking away my negative thoughts and emotions.

SOAR

Gaze up to the sky and keep your eye on a bird. Notice how the bird glides through the air. It works really hard, continuously flapping its wings while finding its direction, and then it soars. After it glides for a while, it rests for a moment and then it begins flapping its wings again, working hard—and then it soars. It glides effortlessly through the sky for a bit and then works hard again, never giving up. You may find it takes a break on a tree branch, only to take flight again once rested. This beautiful animal chooses its direction, knows when to work hard, when to soar, when to rest, and when to take flight again. Birds are free. They have an amazing view of the world and choose to take breaks when their wings are tired. Soar like a bird!

Emotional Identification: Recap

As a teacher, and now a school psychologist, my goal has always been to help children/adolescents identify their emotions and know that they are okay to feel however they are feeling while learning how to process those feelings. This challenging work requires providing strategies to help them manage their emotions rationally and with purpose. I believe that, once you can identify and name an emotion, you can begin to work through it, and it tends to lose power over you. Once you can identify how you feel, you can then process that feeling by validating it and moving through it.

A primary emotion we all need to feel is love; however, that can be blocked. When that happens, you lose sight of other emotions—empathy, kindness, compassion, understanding, trust, honesty, and more. We all need to feel love, be loved, and give love. Whether you did or did not experience unconditional love, you can and do not have to live behind a body of armor. Allow the feeling in and give gratitude for the experience. When love feels foreign and uncomfortable, it makes it difficult to extend it to others, or it becomes forced or unnatural. This can happen even with people in your close circle, such as children, a spouse, and other members of your family. So, unfortunately, the cycle continues. We all need love. It is often easier to give to others rather than to ourselves. You know the saying, "Love the one you're with." That is, *you*. You are with you—always!

Our life experiences help create who we are because they are stored in our memory. Each experience has an emotion or emotions attached to it. Our emotions significantly impact our lives and carve a path for what we do. For example, when we are happy, we typically feel good, so we remember it and probably want to have that experience again. That experience gets stored, so when we remember it or have a similar experience, we feel the emotion all over again—happy. However, when we have an uncomfortable or negative experience and do not process it, acknowledge it, or validate the emotions attached to it, then it is stored that way—uncomfortable. When it creeps back up, we feel that way all over again.

You are in control of your thoughts and emotions, so when you feel something, make sure you can identify the WHY, and if not, do some investigating within yourself to unlock the stored experience that created the emotion you just experienced. This is where you need to use the THINK strategy and remind yourself to Take Hold Immediately Now Knowing you have a purpose and that is to change how you feel and react. This is a process where you will feel those feelings rather than repress them when they arise. To get past them, you must move through them first. If you do not process thoughts, you will remain stuck. No one wants to be stuck. When you are stuck, you are held down as if having an imaginary chain attached to you that you are dragging around along the path of life. It's time to break those chains.

Remember, you become what you think. Thoughts have feelings attached to them and feelings create our moods, so if you can change your thoughts, you can balance your moods. I know what I am saying sounds too simple, but this process really works and causes you to THINK. Let me explain: We often think a lot and even overthink, but is it mindful, purposeful thought? I believe there is a significant difference between the two. Thoughts can be quick, impulsive, irrational; those are the non-mindful thoughts. Thoughts that are processed, present, purposeful, and rational usually have more positive outcomes. More often than not, the non-mindful thoughts, the reactionary ones, just keep us spinning and do not have a positive outcome. It takes a conscious effort and daily practice to THINK purposefully. If it is not something you ordinarily do, it will take time before it becomes automatic.

To improve your well-being, be grateful for who you are, where you are, and what you have. There is a reason for every experience and occurrence in our lives. Think about it, no matter what you have experienced, you got something out of it; there was a consequence, whether positive or negative. There is meaning behind the consequence, although we may not see it at the moment. I undoubtedly believe we are placed in situations with certain people for a reason. In my case, it has been for learning, growing, healing, supporting, and helping others. Remember to practice daily gratitude for yourself and others.

Changes can be beautiful

Afterword

For whatever reason you decided to read this book, thank you. I hope you feel refreshed and ready to love your New Reflection. Love who you are. Do at least one thing every day that makes you happy.

A dream without a goal is just a dream, so set a goal or several goals and turn these few things around:

> Fear into motivation
> > Desperation into inspiration
> > > Fault into responsibility and ownership

Practice daily self-care:

- Exercise—dance, move your body,
- Be mindful,
- Breathe,
- Practice meditation or prayer,
- Self-reflect—journal,
- Draw, paint, crochet,
- Make connections,
- Practice gratitude,
- Find inner peace,
- Live by your personal decree,
- Use daily affirmations,

- Love yourself—give self-hugs, spread kindness, and do something that brings you joy.

Failing is learning. Learning is growing. Growing is changing, and this purposeful change is a choice. Picture a beautiful mountain in front of you with magnificent trees and rocks. You begin to climb towards the top. Once you achieve this great height, you gaze down and see the beauty of the world beneath you. You may trip along the way and get up quickly, but you get up! You may fall hard and fast and have to begin the climb again and again. But you get there, and that is when you stretch out your arms and shout as loud as you can, "I love me, I am free and I am more than enough!" Give yourself a big self-hug, then begin the descent down a whole new you. Head held high, shoulders relaxed—breathe in strength and exhale love.

Remember, in the beginning of the book the plan was to no longer carry the baggage. Now visualize that you are opening your baggage. It is empty and light to hold. Remind yourself, "My past no longer has power over me." Store this as a positive memory, and when you get a negative feeling burdening you, remember this day and tell yourself, my baggage is empty. This is another place you can use THINK. This is a No Dumping zone. Every day is a new day, and some days you will have good moments as well as difficult moments, but you will emerge from those potential traps because your new knowledge will protect you from going down into the abyss. Remember, THINK:

Transformation can happen when I implement my new knowledge. I will Take Hold Immediately Now Knowing. *I am the best version of me!*

Your success is dependent upon you. Work hard for what you want. Integrity—is that one of your values? Are you the same person when no one else is watching? Do you stay true to what you believe in? Self-respect is within you every moment and in every experience you have. To emerge into this new version of you, self-respect is paramount. This goes back to identifying your values, what is important to you, what matters to you. Do not alter your values and beliefs for anyone or anything. Keep boundaries. You must have self-respect first and love who you are, this will radiate through all of your life. No one can give you that. Build a life you do not want to escape from—no more escape rooms to play in. Remember, happiness is not a destination. It is already within you.

To you from me…I hope this is how you feel now:

When I look in the mirror
I love who I see
An amazing person staring back at me
With a radiant smile, unguarded and free
I feel positive energy embedded in my blood
And a freeing spirit within me
As I am free
Free of the pain I carried for far too long
Unveiling the inner me
Beautifully broken but now mended by self-love
Effortlessly, I will be
Living each day with purpose and passion
For I am *Me*

The new reflection you see is from the choices you made to create positive change. Remember, what truly matters in your life is not what you look at but what you see. Soar! Be the wildflower and follow the light.

ABOUT THE AUTHOR

Mary Elizabeth Neils is a licensed New York State school psychologist and former special education teacher who has worked with a diverse population of individuals from early-elementary age to high-school students. She is a mother of two adult boys, and in her spare time she is a fitness professional. Mary Beth holds a Bachelor's degree in Psychology and Elementary Education, a Master's degree in Special Education and a Master's degree in School Psychology. Mary Beth's life's mission has been to support individuals in their quest to: love who they are, take action towards positive change, radiate positivity, and offer kindness and compassion toward themselves and others.

ACKNOWLEDGMENTS

My deepest gratitude to my family for supporting me through the countless hours I spent working on this lifelong dream. To Epigraph Publishing for helping bring my dream into existence, thank you! To my amazing colleague and friend Lindsay for her encouragement and countless conversations about my context. To my mother, father, and brother—without you I would not be me. Together, we found the strength, love, and connection to be resilient and who we are meant to be. I love you with all my heart. To God—for all that I am.

REFERENCES

Allen, James. 1902. *As a Man Thinketh*. New York: Thomas Y. Crowell Company.

Anderson, Lorin W. and David R. Krathwohl. 2000. *A Taxonomy for Learning, Teaching and Assessing: A Revision of Bloom's Taxonomy of Educational Objectives, Complete Edition*. London: Pearson.

Dewey, John. (1933) 1960. *How We Think: A Restatement of The Relation of Reflective Thinking to the Educative Process*. Boston: D. C. Heath and Company.

Frost, Robert. (1914) 1917. "A Servant to Servants." In *North of Boston*. New York: Henry Holt and Company.

Kaufmann, Walter, ed. and trans. (1954) 1976. *The Portable Nietzsche*. New York: Viking Penguin.

Taylor, Thomas, and Floyer Sydenham, eds. and trans. (1804) 2016. *The First Alcibiades: A Dialogue Concerning the Nature of Man (with Taylor's Additional Notes Drawn from the MS Commentary of Proclus)*. Vancouver: Kshetra Books.

Printed in the USA
CPSIA information can be obtained
at www.ICGtesting.com
LVHW040034291023
762449LV00002B/436